A VISUAL GUIDE
TO GOSPEL EVENTS

A VISUAL GUIDE
TO GOSPEL EVENTS

Fascinating Insights into
Where They Happened and Why

JAMES C. MARTIN,
JOHN A. BECK, AND
DAVID G. HANSEN

BakerBooks

a division of Baker Publishing Group
Grand Rapids, Michigan

Published by Baker Books
a division of Baker Publishing Group
P.O. Box 6287, Grand Rapids, MI 49516-6287
www.bakerbooks.com

Printed in the United States of America

Library of Congress Cataloging-in-Publication Data
Martin, James C.
    A visual guide to Gospel events : fascinating insights into where they hap-
pened and why / James C. Martin, John A. Beck, and David G. Hansen.
        p.   cm.
    Includes bibliographical references (p.   ) and index.
    ISBN 978-0-8010-1311-9 (cloth)
    1. Jesus Christ—Travel. 2. Palestine—Description and travel. 3. Bible. N.T.
Gospels—Geography. I. Beck, John A., 1956– II. Hansen, David G., 1938–
III. Title.
BT303.9.M37 2010
232.9′5—dc22   2009038685

Maps by International Mapping

Many locations shown on the maps represent the known ruins of the sites and may not correspond to modern city locations with the same name.

Routes, roads, and regions indicated on the maps are approximate. Buildings, and placement of them in city maps, are representative and approximations of actual locations.

Maps focusing on the Israel/Palestine/Lebanon area were created on an Albers Conic Equal-Area Projection with a central meridian of 35°E and standard parallel at 33°N. The lines of latitude are curved and bend northward at the edges of the subject area.

Maps showing areas outside of Israel were created on an Albers Conic Equal-Area Projection with a central meridian of 40°E and standard parallels at 25°N and 45°N. The lines of latitude are curved and bend northward at the edges of the subject area.

Because of these more correct spatial representations and projections, relative locations on maps in this volume may appear slightly different than on maps in other sources.

The source material for this book is primarily derived from the Bible World Seminars syllabus *Exploring Bible Times*, used in the Bible World Seminars Israel Study Program. For further information on Bible study travel programs in Israel, Egypt, Jordan, Turkey, and Greece, or for information on US seminars, please contact Bible World Seminars (bibleworldseminars@gmail.com).

Photo Credits

All photographs are from the photo archives of Dr. James C. Martin, Bible World Seminars, P.O. Box 2687, Amarillo, TX 79105.

Unless otherwise indicated, photos and illustrations are copyright © Dr. James C. Martin. Additional photo copyrights include: © Direct Design, © Garo Nalbandian, © the Israel Museum and Shrine of the Book, and © the British Museum.

Credits to Those Providing Special Photographic Permissions:

Egypt
The Egyptian Ministry of Antiquities (the Cairo Museum, the Elephantine Museum, the Isma-iliya Museum)
Tombs of the Kings

France
Musée du Louvre; Autorisation de photographer et de filmer—LOUVRE, Paris, France

Greece
The Greek Ministry of Antiquities (Athens, Corinth, Delphi, Thessalonica)

Israel
Collection of the Israel Museum, Jerusalem, and courtesy of the Israel Antiquities Authority, exhibited at the Israel Museum, Jerusalem
Collection of the Israel Museum, Jerusalem, and courtesy of the Israel Antiquities Authority, exhibited at the Shrine of the Book, the Israel Museum, Jerusalem
Collection of the Israel Museum, Jerusalem, and courtesy of the Israel Antiquities Authority, exhibited at the Rockefeller Museum, Jerusalem
The Eretz Israel Museum, Tel Aviv, Israel
The House of Anchors Museum, Kibbutz Ein Gev, Sea of Galilee, Israel
Garo Nalbandian
Nazareth Church of Annunciation
Reproduction of the City of Jerusalem at the time of the Second Temple—located on the grounds of the Holyland Hotel, Jerusalem, 2001. Present location: The Israel Museum, Jerusalem. Photographed by permission.
The Skirball Museum, Hebrew Union College—Jewish Institute of Religion, 13 King David Street, Jerusalem 94101

The Yigal Allon Centre, Kibbutz Ginosar, on the western shore of the Sea of Galilee, Israel
The Wohl Archaeological Museum and Burnt House, Jerusalem

Italy
The Italian Ministry of Antiquities: On licence Ministero per I Beni e le Attivita Culturali—Soprintendenza Archaeologica di Roma, Rome, Italy

Jordan
The Jordanian Ministry of Antiquities (the Amman Archaeological Museum, the Jerash Archaeological Museum)

Turkey
The Turkish Ministry of Antiquities (the Ankara Museum, the Antalya Museum, the Aphrodisias Museum, the Ephesus Museum, the Haytay Museum, the Hierapolis Museum, the Konya Museum, the Manisa Museum, the Istanbul Archaeological Museum)

United Kingdom
The British Museum, London, England

United States
Direct Design
Sola Scriptura—the Van Kampen Collection on display at the Holy Land Experience, Orlando, Florida

---

Interior design by Brian Brunsting

CONTENTS

ACKNOWLEDGMENTS

A very special thanks to all who have participated in Bible World Seminars' overseas Bible study programs. Without your involvement, desire of adventure, and excitement for studying Scripture in its original location, this project would not have been possible. A grateful acknowledgment and thanks goes also to Bruce Bordine, Dick Brooks, Carolyn Hansen, Dixie and Gray Keller, Marvin Martin, Linda McGinness, and Allison Northern, who have worked with and supported Bible World Seminars throughout the years. Additional thanks to Timothy Ladwig for his work on the illustrations, Dr. Carl Rasmussen for recommending this project, and all those at Baker Publishing Group who made it possible.

PART 1

THE BIRTH AND EARLY YEARS OF JESUS

Woman gathering wheat stalks.

The Bible makes known the most extensive rescue in the history of the world. It reveals God's perspective of the human condition and his plan to liberate and restore creation from discord, destruction, and death—all consequences of humanity's mutiny against the Lord.

The Bible unfolds an interconnected flow of this rescue. Genesis chapters 1–11 introduce us to the reality of the adversary, Satan, his cohorts, humanity's willful rejection of its Creator, and the world's desperate need for a rescuer. Genesis 12 through the book of Malachi speaks of a nation chosen to be messengers the Lord called to proclaim the coming of the Rescuer. The four Gospels of Matthew, Mark, Luke, and John provide the accounts of the Rescuer's arrival.[1] In Hebrew, his name is *Yeshua*, which means "the Lord rescues." Our English Bibles refer to him as Jesus. Through his teachings, miracles, death, and resurrection, he overthrew the adversary and his works (1 John 3:8) as well as rescued and restored humanity's relationship with the Creator of the universe (Rom. 5:10–11; 2 Cor. 5:17–21).

These events of rescue and restoration occurred in a localized space that today we call Israel, Palestine, the Promised Land, and the Holy Land. The goal of this book is to show the important relationship between the events and teachings of Jesus and the places they occurred. Those events happened where they did for a reason.

Part 1 starts our journey with the birth and early years of Jesus. We will examine some events and places that are well known to the Bible reader and many that are less familiar. For example, we will see that the Gospel of Matthew introduces us to Jesus by taking us to a public archive. We will explore the relationship between the birth announcement the angel Gabriel gave to the father of John the Baptist and the place where his father was standing at the time. It is well known that Mary and Joseph lived in Nazareth, but some have never considered the significance of this location and perhaps why they lived there. In that light, we will explore Mary's journey from her home in Nazareth to be with Elizabeth for three months in the hill country of Judea. Many details associated with Jesus's birth are known to us. Exploring relationships between events and places will take us to the guest room that was unavailable, the manger in the cave, and the shepherds in the fields.

Following Jesus's birth, the Gospel writers mention few details about his early life, and the details they do record are often connected to a particular place. Consequently, we will reflect on the presentation of the infant Jesus at the Temple's Nicanor Gate, the appearance of the star in the east, and the delay of Jesus at the Temple when he was twelve years old. All these events, and more, happened where they did for a reason.

Assyrian genealogy of Adad-nirari III (810–783 BC).

Basement-cave under a Judean house.

As an infant, Jesus was taken to Nicanor Gate in the Court of Women to be dedicated by the priests.

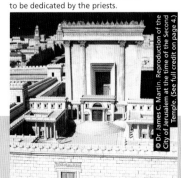

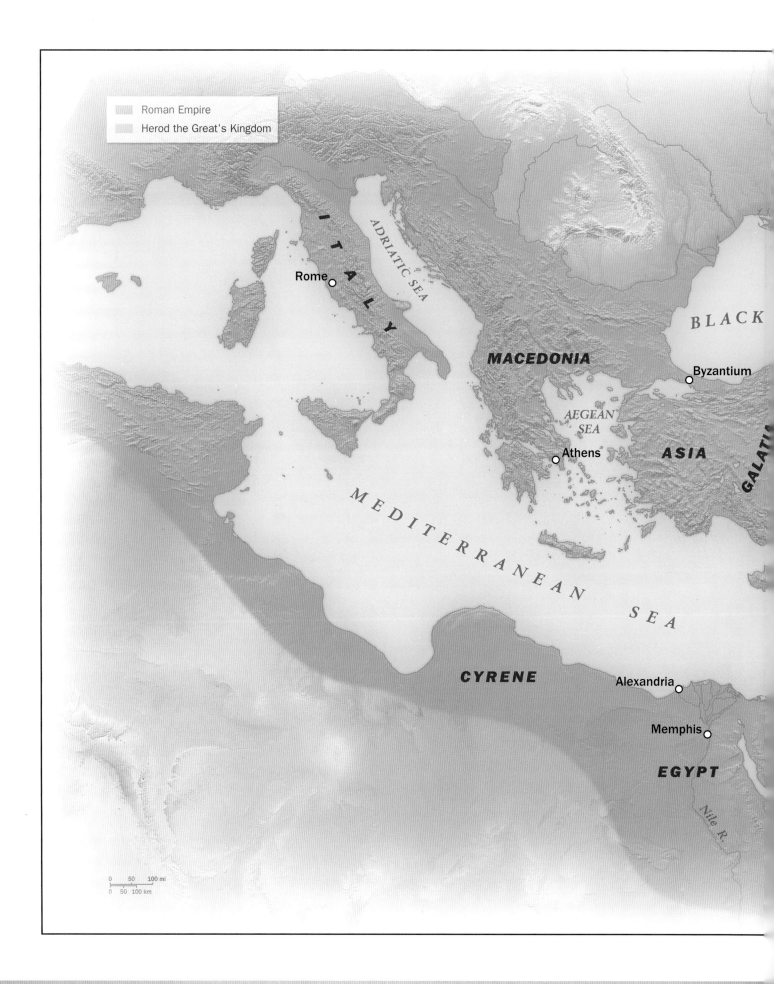

Roman Empire

Herod the Great's Kingdom

I T A L Y

ADRIATIC SEA

Rome

MACEDONIA

BLACK

Byzantium

AEGEAN SEA

Athens

ASIA

GALATIA

M E D I T E R R A N E A N   S E A

CYRENE

Alexandria

Memphis

EGYPT

Nile R.

0   50   100 mi

0   50 100 km

N

SEA

CASPIAN SEA

CILICIA

Antioch

SYRIA

Euphrates R.

Tigris R.

PARTHIAN EMPIRE

Jordan R.

Jerusalem

ARABIA

PERSIAN GULF

ED SEA

GENEALOGICAL REGISTERS AT PUBLIC ARCHIVES

MATTHEW 1:1–17

In first-century Judaism, genealogical registers were physical records that provided essential cultural information.[2] In order to know how to function in Israelite society—especially regarding issues pertaining to priestly heritage, marriage considerations, social status, religious assignments, and political authority—people had to know family heritage.[3]

Thus, in the period of the Gospels written records listing the descendants of Abraham, Isaac, and Jacob were collected and secured in buildings designated for public records.[4] In the case of priestly heritage, each member of Israel's priesthood was required to trace his genealogy to the tribe of Levi. He could become a legitimate high priest only if he was also a descendant of the family of Aaron (Num. 3:1–13). The Israelite priesthood also kept an official genealogical register at the Temple.[5] That way a background check on those who aspired to the priesthood could be done easily by inspecting this public record.

Marriage considerations were of particular concern to all Israelites of pure blood. If a priest wanted his son to be eligible for the priesthood, the son had to marry a woman of priestly

Illustration of scribes working with genealogical records.

descent, tracing her family from a verifiably accurate genealogical register back through several generations of mothers on both sides of the family.[6] Israelites not of the priestly line were also concerned about knowing their heritage because only certain groups could intermarry.[7] Moreover, to marry outside of the extended-family system could put the assets of the family at risk.

Social status was also verified through genealogical registers. The famous Jewish historian Josephus bragged that his genealogical register revealed his high social status.[8] Others, however, had to bear humiliation when occurrences of disgrace were denoted in their genealogical register. The Jewish oral law known as the Mishnah records that Rabbi Simeon Ben Azzai said, "I found a family register in Jerusalem and in it was written,

Palmyra tomb sculpture providing a genealogy of the deceased.

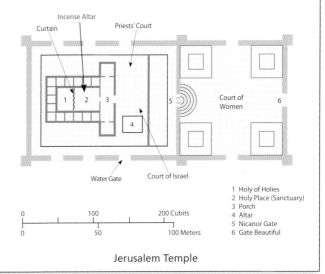

Jerusalem Temple

1 Holy of Holies
2 Holy Place (Sanctuary)
3 Porch
4 Altar
5 Nicanor Gate
6 Gate Beautiful

Model depicting a first-century Jerusalem archive building used to hold legal documents, including genealogical registers.

© Dr. James C. Martin. Reproduction of the City of Jerusalem at the time of the Second Temple. (See full credit on page 4.)

'Such-a-one is a bastard through [a transgression of the law of] thy neighbor's wife.'"[9]

Israelites also had various Temple assignments associated with family heritage (Neh. 10:34). Those from the tribe of Judah and house of David, including Joseph (Mary's husband), were to bring the wood offering to the Temple on the twenty-fifth day of Tammuz.[10]

Political authority was also closely related to family lineage. Only someone of Israelite heritage could legitimately claim the title of king (Deut. 17:14–15). When Herod the Great came to the throne, his illegitimate rule was obvious to all. According to the ancient historian Eusebius, Herod had "no drop of Israelitish blood in his veins and was stung by the consciousness of his base origin, [so] he burnt the registers of [the Israelites'] families."[11]

In that context Matthew begins his Gospel with a trip to the public archives. Questions related to a person's lineage within Jewish society were resolved through examination of genealogical registers found in public archives. Therefore, opponents of Jesus used the public records to challenge the fact that he could be the Messiah (John 8:41). Others, like Luke, use the genealogical records to verify Jesus's legitimacy as Messiah (Luke 3:23–38).

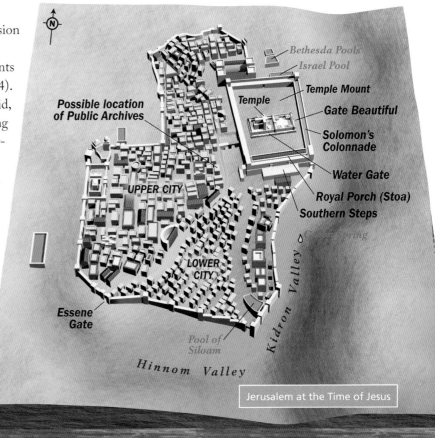

Jerusalem at the Time of Jesus

ZECHARIAH AT THE ALTAR OF INCENSE

LUKE 1:8–22

John the Baptist was given a special responsibility: to prepare Israel to meet the Messiah (Mal. 3:1). Jesus even made note of John's importance (Luke 7:28). So it is fitting that this man, John, had a birth accompanied by prophetic clarification. Here we will explore the possibility of why the angel Gabriel announced the coming birth of John to his father, the priest Zechariah, at the altar of incense in the sanctuary of the Temple.

It was the descendants of Aaron who had the task of serving at the Temple, but at the time of the Gospels there were too many priests to have them all working in the Temple at one time. As a result, they were divided into twenty-four courses, or divisions, that served in rotation (1 Chron. 24:1–19). Those on duty in Jerusalem led God's people in worship and tended the Temple altars, including the altar of incense inside the Temple building. This special altar was located in the Holy Place, directly in front of the curtain that separated the Holy Place from the Holy of Holies, where the Ark of the Covenant was kept. No one but a priest was allowed into the Holy Place, and then only when a special duty was assigned—like tending to the coals and incense on the altar of incense.[12] This specific duty was so special that those who fulfilled this responsibility on any given day were selected by lot. Once a priest was so chosen and honored, he never had the chance to do so again.[13]

Unlike the counterfeit chief priests from the party of the Sadducees who controlled the Temple and its activities at that time, Zechariah was a true priest from the division of Abijah (Luke 1:5). Zechariah's division was called for duty, and because this priestly selection process held true, for the only time in his life, at his advanced age, Zechariah was selected for the honor of tending the altar of incense (Luke 1:8–10).[14]

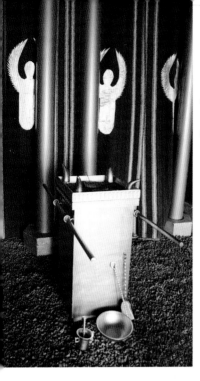

Model of the outer sanctuary of the tabernacle, depicting the incense altar and curtain used to separate the Ark of the Covenant in the Holy of Holies.

Model of the Temple and Court of Women (foreground) and Court of Israel (background). Late in his life, Zechariah was finally chosen by lot to enter the sanctuary and carry out his priestly duties.

But behind the joy of this day lay the disappointment he and his wife, Elizabeth, experienced because they had been unable to have children (Luke 1:7, 57–58). This was about to change, for as Zechariah entered the Temple sanctuary and tended the incense altar, the angel Gabriel appeared to him with incredible news. Not only would he and his wife have a son, but this son would also be the forerunner of the promised Messiah (Luke 1:17; Mal. 4:5–6).

This was incredible news no matter where Gabriel announced it, but Luke is very careful to note that this announcement came to Zechariah as Gabriel stood "at the right side of the altar of incense" (Luke 1:11). The smoke rising from this altar symbolized the prayers of God's people rising before him.[15] Gabriel made the connection between this place and the announcement by noting that Zechariah's prayer requesting a son was answered (Luke 1:13).

So it was that while in the inner sanctuary of the Temple, the place where prayers ascended to God, the angel Gabriel brought Zechariah the wonderful news of his promised son who would prepare the way of the Lord. This faithful priest joined other prophets—such as David, Isaiah, Jeremiah, Joel, and Malachi—when he was filled with the Holy Spirit and began prophesying about his own son's participation in the coming of the Rescuer-Redeemer (Luke 1:67–79; see also Ps. 16:8–11; Isaiah 53; Jer. 23:5; Joel 2:28–32; Acts 2:16–32).

◄ Model of Jerusalem's Temple complex in the first century.

This four-horned limestone incense altar (975–925 BC) from Megiddo dates to the time of King Solomon. Incense altars were also used in the Temple.

MOVING FROM JUDEA

LUKE 1:26–27

In first-century Israel it was typical for families to live their entire lives in the same region and even the same village. That fact makes the lives of Mary and Joseph in Nazareth somewhat unusual since each of their families had roots in the region of Judea. Although the Gospel writers do not discuss why the families moved from Judea, we can offer evidence that suggests each family made its move for a reason.

The evidence of Joseph's family coming from Judea is that when the Roman government demanded that the Israelites register their family property for tax purposes, Joseph traveled to Bethlehem of Judea because his family origin was from Bethlehem, the town of David (Luke 2:1–5). We know that Mary had family in Judea because she traveled to the hill country of Judea in order to visit her relatives (Luke 1:36, 39–40). We also know that Joseph's and Mary's immediate families had moved north to Nazareth because Luke states that the angel Gabriel came "to Nazareth, a town in Galilee," and announced to Mary that she would be the mother of the Messiah (Luke 1:26). Furthermore, Luke notes that Joseph and Mary left for Bethlehem from Nazareth (Luke 2:4).

So why had these families moved to Nazareth? For Mary, we turn to a fragment of an inscription discovered in 1962 that lists priestly families from Judea who had settled in the Galilee prior to the time of the Gospels in order to await the coming Messiah.[16]

In 24–15 BC Herod the Great conscripted workers from nearby villages such as Bethlehem to build the Herodium, the palace-fortress-tomb named after himself.

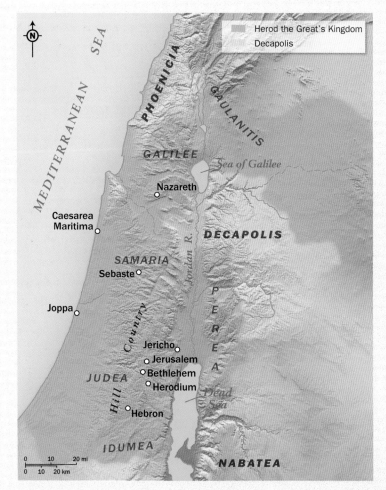

Kingdom of Herod the Great

This may explain why Mary had to travel to Judea to visit with her priestly Judean relatives, Zechariah and Elizabeth (Luke 1:5).

In the case of Joseph's family, we look to Israel's political climate at the end of the first century BC when violence and corruption escalated in the region of Judea. The Romans had conquered the Promised Land and ruled it through their puppet king, Herod the Great, whom the Roman senate declared "King of the Jews." Herod's tenure as king was marked by his oppressive unpredictability.[17] No one knew exactly what to expect from him, and even his own family members were murdered when he felt threatened by their popularity. In this light, Roman Emperor Augustus quipped that it was better to be one of Herod's pigs than one of his sons.[18]

Moreover, in his fear of invasions from the east, Herod built numerous fortifications including the Herodium, which was of particular concern to observant Jews living in Bethlehem. Herod had it constructed about 24–15 BC only three and a half miles southeast of this village.[19] Since Joseph worked in the building trade (Matt. 13:55), there may have been reason for him to leave Bethlehem to avoid being conscripted into Herod's building program.

The inner complex of the Herodium consisted of a dining hall, a bath complex, gardens, and living quarters.

Families, like those of Mary and Joseph, who were dedicated to living the lifestyle God had planned for the Israelites, abhorred the immoral rule of Herod.[20] Consequently, many chose to withdraw from the region of Judea to remote villages in the Galilee like Nazareth—a small agricultural village that was most noteworthy because it was so little worthy of note. There Mary and Joseph insulated themselves from the corrupt Roman culture that had even permeated the walls of the Temple while awaiting the arrival of the Messiah, who would restore rightful leadership in the land.[21]

Herod the Great built the Herodium about three miles southeast of Bethlehem.

ENCOURAGEMENT FROM WOMEN IN THE HILL COUNTRY

LUKE 1:39–56

The good news of great joy brought by the angel Gabriel must have prompted in Mary recurring thoughts and questions about what this announcement meant (Luke 1:26–35). In the days after learning that she would conceive the Son of God by the Holy Spirit, Mary left Nazareth and departed for the hill country of Judea for a reason.

Following Gabriel's visit, Mary probably wondered how her family and community would receive the news of her pregnancy. She was "pledged to be married to . . . Joseph" (Luke 1:27). Like other matches within her Jewish culture, Mary's betrothal was a legal contract that carried with it numerous expectations.[22] During the time between their betrothal contract and formal marriage, the couple was considered husband and wife. Although there is no indication in the Bible, it was common within the culture for the girl to be married by thirteen and the man by eighteen to twenty.[23] Contact between the couple was strictly prohibited, and sexual relations prior to the wedding could result in their execution.[24]

Mary had entered a betrothal agreement that was considered a legal marriage contract, and she had not engaged in sexual relations (Luke 1:27, 34). Yet she was pregnant and so would be considered unfaithful to her marriage contract, which made it probable that Joseph would divorce her because of her perceived unfaithfulness (Matt. 1:19). Potentially, both she and her baby would struggle to survive as social outcasts, and she even faced the possibility of execution (Deut. 22:23–24).[25]

It is no wonder that "Mary got ready and hurried to a town in the hill country of Judea" (Luke 1:39) to visit her relative, Elizabeth, a woman who knew something

© Direct Design.

Mary traveled from the region of Galilee to Judea in order to meet with her relative Elizabeth.

Ein Kerem. It is believed by some that Elizabeth and Zechariah lived at Ein Kerem, a village near Jerusalem's western suburbs.

about disgrace. Elizabeth had felt the sting of social humiliation because she was childless (Luke 1:7, 25). Her long wait for a child was rewarded, and she gave birth to John, the forerunner of the Messiah. The angel Gabriel had earlier told Mary that Elizabeth was six months along in her pregnancy (Luke 1:36–37). Thus Mary found reassurance from Elizabeth—a family member who lived in the hill country.

Mary shared her experience with Elizabeth, who was also participating in the miraculous unfolding of God's rescue and restoration of humanity. Mary received and gave reassurance as she greeted Elizabeth. At the sound of Mary's greeting, Elizabeth's baby leaped within her. Then Elizabeth, filled with the Holy Spirit, blessed Mary for believing that the Lord would do what he had said (Luke 1:41–45), and Mary praised God in a song that celebrated the way he takes the humble and exalts them (Luke 1:46–55).

This song holds a note of victory that is reminiscent of Hannah's joyful song hundreds of years earlier (1 Sam. 2:1–10). Hannah came from a village in the hill country of Ephraim, a few miles north of Jerusalem, and like Elizabeth, she had been childless for years and felt the brunt of social ostracism (1 Sam. 1:3–8). But God announced to her that she would give birth to Samuel, who grew up to become the prophet of Israel who anointed David as king (1 Sam. 1:17–20; 16:13).

So it was that Elizabeth and Hannah saw their social disgrace give way to honor. Both lived in the hill country where Mary found reassurance as she pondered the wondrous ways of God.[26]

Ramah. Hannah came from the village of Ramah, about eight miles north of Bethlehem.

Early second-century marriage contract, known as a *ketubah*, discovered in the Judean desert among the archives of Babata.

NO ROOM IN THE GUEST ROOM
LUKE 2:6–7

Both Matthew and Luke write that Jesus was born in Bethlehem (Matt. 2:1; Luke 2:1–7). This detail is significant because that is exactly where God promised the Messiah would be born (Mic. 5:2). But Luke considers it just as important to tell us where Jesus was *not* born. He was not born in a palace, hotel, or even a guest room (Luke 2:7). We will explore both the language Luke uses to describe where Jesus was born and the reason there was no room in the guest room for Mary and Joseph.

A Bethlehem home was commonly built over a cave and had only two rooms, each with distinctive functions. The larger room was the family's daily living space where they cooked their meals and rolled out their sleeping mats. The smaller room (Greek, *kataluma*) was a storage room that could be made available to accommodate family or friends who visited overnight.[27] Necessary livestock was kept in the cave below the home. Luke reports that when Joseph and Mary arrived in Bethlehem there was no room in the guest room (*kataluma*;

In first-century Bethlehem, homes were usually built over a basement-cave, with sleeping, cooking, storage, and a guest room on the top level.

In first-century Bethlehem, houses such as this one were constructed with limestone.

Luke 2:7), so they ended up in the basement-cave of the house.

Some might wonder, "What happened to the inn?" Many Christians have grown up with a Bible translation that says, "There was no room for them in the inn." It is unlikely, however, that this is what Luke intends when the Greek text of the Gospels and the Hebrew culture of first-century Judea are considered. The Greek word for a traveler's inn is *pandocheion*. Luke uses this word later when he describes the inn where the Good Samaritan took the injured man (Luke 10:34). But this is not the word Luke uses for the place in Bethlehem that had no room for Joseph and Mary.

He writes that there was no room in the *kataluma*—a word that describes the guest room of a house. Cultural expectations point to the likelihood that when Mary and Joseph arrived in Bethlehem, they would have gone to the home of an extended family member or village patriarch and asked to use their guest room for the night.

Since Luke does not tell us why there was no room in the guest room, we are curious to inspect the circumstances to explain why Mary and Joseph were staying in the place livestock were kept. First, there must have been others in Bethlehem from out of town because the Romans had demanded everyone go to "his own town" for the census (Luke 2:3; see vv. 1–3). Therefore, one possibility for denying them the guest room was that Bethlehem was already crowded with those coming to register their family property. Thus the guest rooms may have been claimed already by other families.[28]

Another option can be found in the culture of first-century Judaism. Leviticus 12:1–4 makes it clear that when a baby was born the mother became ritually unclean. Her status of ritual impurity also put the condition of the house and its contents at risk of becoming ritually unclean. The stone cave under the house, however, functioned as a screen against the transmission of ritual uncleanness.[29] Therefore, remaining in the basement-cave may have been Mary and Joseph's decision in order to prevent ritual impurity from affecting the entire house.

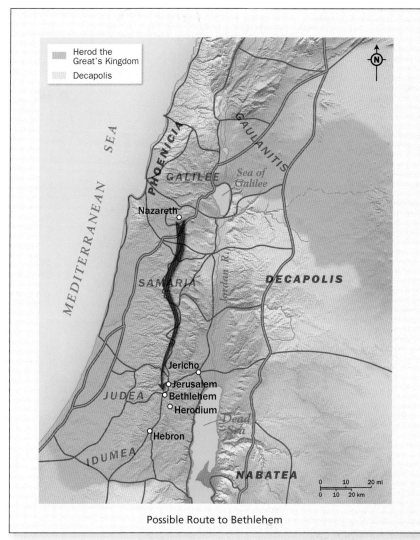

Possible Route to Bethlehem

The guest room (Greek, *kataluma*) of a Judean house.

MARY PLACES JESUS IN A MANGER

LUKE 2:7, 12, 16

Only Luke's Gospel provides us with images of the events surrounding the initial hours of the birth of Jesus in which God came to dwell with us. It is not by coincidence that Luke repeats three times that on this special day Jesus was placed in a manger. As a practical matter, we may find Jesus in the manger because it was convenient. Far more important was the powerful message sent to Israel when Jesus was placed in a manger.

Because the guest rooms in the Bethlehem homes were not available, Joseph and Mary lodged in the next best shelter under the circumstances. In those days, family homes usually had a small collection of animals that provided them with meat, milk, labor, and fertilizer. Because predators prowled the fields during the night, families brought their animals in to a shelter for safekeeping. In Bethlehem that

Thatched feeding trough in a basement-cave.

shelter was often a natural cave that either was incorporated into the home as its basement or was close enough to the family's home to make it a safe haven.[30] It was in just such a humble setting that Mary gave birth to Jesus. Because the animals were fed in the cave, feeding troughs known as mangers were placed in the shelter. Thus a manger made of mud or stone was in the animal shelter and could be used as a bed for the newborn King.

When Mary wrapped her infant son in swaddling cloths and placed him in a manger, she sent the Lord's message to Israel about the nation's relationship with God. That is why Luke mentions the manger not once but three times in relating the events of this special day (Luke 2:7, 12, 16). Gabriel had told Mary that her son would be great, would be called the "Son of the Most High," and would sit on the throne of David (Luke 1:32). Normally such a monarch was born in a royal setting, yet we find the Rescuer of the world lying in a feeding trough.

Although mangers were a common feature of first-century Bethlehem, they were not ordinarily used as a

Cow feeding at a feeding trough (manger) constructed of mud.

Fourth-century sarcophagus of the infant Jesus wrapped in a swaddling cloth and placed in a manger.

bed for an infant, and certainly not for an infant with royal blood flowing in his veins. Mangers, however, were used in the prophetic imagery of Isaiah to describe Israel's ignorance in their understanding of God: "Hear O heavens! Listen, O earth! For the LORD has spoken: . . . 'The ox knows his master, the donkey his owner's manger, but Israel does not know, my people do not understand'" (Isa. 1:2–3).

In accordance with Isaiah's message, Luke records the birth of our Savior as unattended by kings, priests, prophets, rabbis, or scribes. Yet Israel was called to come to the Messiah, signified by Mary as she laid her baby in the manger. Jesus in the manger—like the food in the feeding trough—would be Israel's nourishment. Yet would Israel understand well enough to recognize the Anointed One?

Stone feeding trough (eighth century BC) from the stables of Megiddo.

SHEPHERDS IN THE BETHLEHEM FIELDS

LUKE 2:8–20

God would not allow the birth of his Son to go without praise, recognition, and celebration! So after the darkness of night set in, he sent angels to shepherds who were watching their flocks in the nearby agricultural fields of Bethlehem (Hebrew for "house of bread") so that the praise to God for the Messiah's arrival might commence (Luke 2:8–14).

Several pieces of evidence in Luke's Gospel help us understand the events surrounding this angelic birth announcement.[31] First, these shepherds were staying in the agricultural fields (Greek, *agruleo*). Those who spend time on or near a farm are aware of the importance of keeping livestock separated from field crops. Our assumption is that the people in Bethlehem would have a similar concern—particularly since Bethlehem was famous for its grain fields—so we do not expect to see livestock in these grain fields before the harvest or times of sowing. However, when the harvest was complete, the shepherds were welcome to bring their animals into the fields so they could nose through the stubble for leftover kernels the harvesters had missed. In return, the sheep left behind valuable manure that improved the quality of the soil, increasing the yield of those fields in the following season.[32] Thus after harvest, it is no surprise to find shepherds with their flocks in the agricultural fields located just east of Bethlehem.[33]

Our curiosity rises, however, when we note that Luke's Gospel mentions that the shepherds to whom the angels announced Jesus's birth were "keeping watch over their flocks at night" (Luke 2:8). Typically sheep and goats grazed during the day and were brought into sheepfolds for the night. The unusual conduct of the shepherds who were in the field rather than a sheepfold at night may indicate that they were not ordinary shepherds but Temple shepherds in charge of the flocks that were destined for sacrifice.[34] Those flocks required continuous supervision in order to ensure their unblemished quality.[35]

The fact that the Lord assigned an angelic proclamation of the Messiah's birth to a group of shepherds—regardless of whether they were ordinary shepherds or Temple herdsmen—is surprising since in first-century Judaism being a shepherd was considered a despised vocation. Shepherds who were adults were probably hired to take care of another person's flock. Otherwise the task fell to the youngest members of the family or the women (see 1 Sam. 16:8–13; 17:12–30). The vocation was particularly

Shepherd near Bethlehem taking care of his goat.

Shepherd riding a donkey, leading his flock.

frowned on because it was thought to be a job taken up by thieves. As a result, rabbinic law forbade people from buying by-products of sheep or goats directly from a shepherd.[36]

Rather than making the announcement of the Messiah's birth to the rich and famous, the angel delivered this great news to those considered outcasts, who were doing the undesirable night duty in the harvested grain fields near Bethlehem. After the angel told them the amazing news that the Messiah had been born nearby and the angelic chorus filled the night with praises to God, these shepherds went to find the newborn King, Jesus. They found Mary and Joseph and the baby, who was lying in the manger. After seeing the baby, the shepherds spread the word of the newborn King and returned to their flocks "glorifying and praising God for all the things they had heard and seen" (Luke 2:20).

The Messiah was to be born of a virgin (Isa. 7:14) in Bethlehem (Mic. 5:2). And it was to shepherds in the agricultural fields east of Bethlehem that the angels of God proclaimed the Messiah's arrival, personally inviting them to meet the Bread of Life, who was born in Bethlehem, the "house of bread."

Shepherdess outside Bethlehem.

THE REDEEMER AT THE TEMPLE

LUKE 2:22–38

After Jesus's birth, he, Joseph, and Mary remained in Bethlehem for over a month before journeying the five and a half miles to the Temple in Jerusalem (Lev. 12:4; Luke 2:22). For the first time this place, so filled with imagery representing the Messiah, actually experienced his presence. Luke records that Joseph and Mary were at the Temple not only for her purification but also to present Jesus to a priest who would dedicate him at the ceremony of the redemption of the firstborn son (Luke 2:22–24).

Following Mary's purification and offering, Joseph and Mary brought Jesus to the Temple's Nicanor Gate[37] that opened from the Court of Israel to the Court of Women at the top of fifteen, semicircular steps. This place was set aside for ceremonies that were to be done before the Lord, including parents bringing their firstborn sons to be redeemed in remembrance of God's deliverance of ancient Israel from Egyptian bondage (Exod. 13:2–3). This captivity had come to an end with

Illustration of Mary's purification at the Temple after the birth of Jesus.

a plague that took the life of every firstborn Egyptian son (Exodus 11). In gratitude that Israel's firstborn sons were spared the fate of the Egyptians, every firstborn Israelite male was to be presented to God soon after his birth so that he might be redeemed (Exod. 34:19). A brief ceremony was held to remind Israel of God's saving act, which was referred to as "redemption." In this ceremony a priest pronounced two blessings: one giving thanks for the birth of the child and the other celebrating his redemption. After the offering was given, the ceremony was over.[38]

Although Joseph and Mary had brought Jesus to the Temple and completed the ceremony, something was missing. The priest had done his part, but he did not recognize that Jesus was the promised Messiah. What the priest had not seen was clearly acknowledged by

The Temple Mount (aerial view looking north). The main entrance onto the Temple Mount, located at the bottom of the photo, was where Joseph and Mary entered the Temple complex with the infant Jesus.

two other faithful servants of God, Simeon and Anna, who made the public proclamation of Jesus as the Redeemer of Israel.

The first, Simeon, was an old man who had been given a special promise. God had told him that he would not die before seeing the promised Messiah (Luke 2:25–26). Prompted by the Holy Spirit, Simeon entered the Temple courts, took Jesus in his arms, and praised God saying, "My eyes have seen your salvation, which you have prepared in the sight of all people, a light for revelation to the Gentiles and for glory to your people Israel" (Luke 2:30–32; see also Isa. 42:6–7; 49:6; Acts 4:12).

Next there was an elderly prophetess at the Temple, Anna, who had been waiting many years in the Temple courts for the arrival of the Messiah. When she saw the infant and heard Simeon's blessing, she gave thanks to God and talked about the baby Jesus to all who were looking for the redemption of Jerusalem (Luke 2:36–38). Thus Mary and Joseph brought Jesus to the Nicanor Gate to perform the ceremony to redeem Jesus. But the Father used this occasion to announce in the Temple that this child, this light to the nations (John 8:12), would redeem the world.

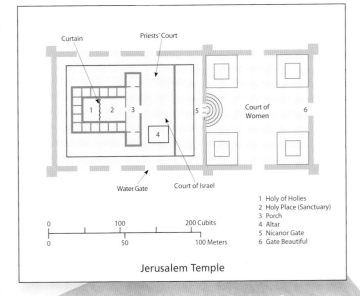

1 Holy of Holies
2 Holy Place (Sanctuary)
3 Porch
4 Altar
5 Nicanor Gate
6 Gate Beautiful

Jerusalem Temple

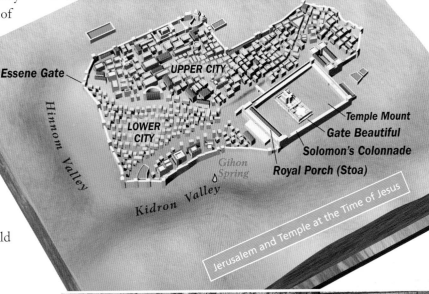

Jerusalem and Temple at the Time of Jesus

Scuola Nuova tapestry (AD 1524–31) depicting the presentation at the Temple.

MAGI FOLLOW THE STAR

MATTHEW 2:1–12

Following the birth of Jesus, Mary and Joseph remained in Bethlehem. It was during those months that they welcomed special visitors who brought very expensive gifts for Jesus. A star led the Magi, sometimes called the Wise Men, to the place where Jesus's family was staying. We will explore possibilities of the identity of the Magi and the meaning associated with the star that led them.[39]

The English word *Magi* is a transliteration of the Greek word *magoi*. Its traditional use comes from the Greek translation of the Hebrew Old Testament known as the Septuagint. The Greek word *magos* in Daniel 2 verses 2 and 10 in the Septuagint is a translation of the Hebrew word *ash-shaph*, which is usually applied to those who are involved in the practice of magic and sorcery. Because the Magi in Matthew's Gospel were following a star to find Jesus, it is sometimes assumed these men were astrologers. There are, however, troubling elements with respect to such an interpretation. In the first place, all acts of divination, including astrology, were strictly forbidden in Scripture and rabbinic literature (Deut. 18:10–12; Mishnah, *Sanhedrin* 7:11). It is problematic that Gentile astrologers would be looking for a Jewish Messiah, but it is more inconceivable that an observant Jewish couple like Joseph and Mary would allow agents of sorcery into

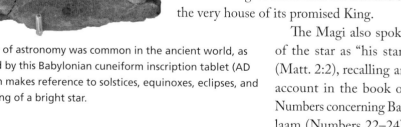

© Dr. James C. Martin. The British Museum. Photographed by permission.

The study of astronomy was common in the ancient world, as evidenced by this Babylonian cuneiform inscription tablet (AD 61), which makes reference to solstices, equinoxes, eclipses, and the sighting of a bright star.

their home. It is plausible the Magi who are reported in Matthew's Gospel may not have been astrologers but rather descendants of exiled Jews in the east who were wise in the knowledge of God.

Whether the Magi from the east who came to honor Jesus were Jews or Gentiles, Daniel's place of prominence in the court and among the magi in Babylon suggests he or other Jewish exiles may have taught of the Messiah's coming. So when the star appeared, some among the magi may have recognized it for what it was and followed it.

There are other interesting elements of the star and the coming of the Magi that suggest scriptural connections. For example, the star functioned in much the same way as the pillar of cloud and the pillar of fire that guided Moses and the children of Israel to the Promised Land (Exod. 13:21–22). In a similar way the star led the Magi to the Promised Land and to the very house of its promised King.

The Magi also spoke of the star as "his star" (Matt. 2:2), recalling an account in the book of Numbers concerning Balaam (Numbers 22–24). He was a prophet of divination from Pethor along the Euphrates River who was hired by the king of Moab to curse Israel. Instead he blessed Israel and predicted God would raise up a Jewish king who would rule over the nations. Balaam said it would be the image of the star that

Star in Bethlehem's Church of the Nativity, commemorating the location of the birth of Jesus.

Magi Follow the Star

represented this political authority: "I see him, but not now; I behold him, but not near. A star will come out of Jacob; a scepter will rise out of Israel" (Num. 24:17).

We do not know whether the star was a purely supernatural manifestation of the glory of God—like the pillars of cloud and of fire of the exodus experience (Exod. 13:22)—or was a providential orchestration of natural events linked to the birth of the Messiah.[40] What we do know is that long before Jesus gave his first teaching or chose his first disciple, God set a star in the east to lead men from distant lands to find and worship the Messiah who had been born in Bethlehem.

Sarcophagus lid from Rome (fourth century), depicting the adoration of the Magi.

Silver coin of the Parthian ruler Vologases I (AD 51–78).

REMAINING BEHIND
AT THE TEMPLE

LUKE 2:43–52

Words fail to describe the fear and worry that washes over a mother and father when their child is missing. Parents can identify with the fear and worry Mary and Joseph experienced when they left Jerusalem for their six-day journey back to Galilee only to find they had lost contact with Jesus.[41] Upon realizing he was missing, they returned to Jerusalem to search for him and ultimately found him in the Temple. The Gospel of Luke makes it clear that this separation was not accidental. Jesus remained behind at the Temple for a reason.

As God had directed, Jesus and his family traveled from their home in Nazareth to Jerusalem in order to observe the Passover (Luke 2:41).[42] Luke goes on to note that this Passover was a special time for Jesus. He was twelve years old (Luke 2:42)—one year away from his Bar Mitzvah. On this trip to the Temple he may have observed other

Throughout history, Jewish pilgrims from around the world have gathered in the area of Jerusalem's Temple to celebrate various festivals.

Bar Mitzvahs and had his own vows examined in advance of his confirmation the following year.[43]

Prayer and study at the western wall of the Temple Mount.

Everything went according to plan until Mary and Joseph headed home. The caravan departed Jerusalem for Galilee and made camp at the end of the first day of travel. It was only then that Joseph and Mary discovered Jesus was not with them. We might be shocked that neither Mary nor Joseph realized Jesus was missing until an entire day elapsed, but there is a likely explanation. People typically traveled in caravans, with men and women in separate groups; men guarded the caravan while the women cared for the children and animals. Perhaps Jesus had traveled to Jerusalem in the company of Mary. Upon their return, Mary assumed Jesus, who had just finished his pre–Bar Mitzvah overview, was now traveling with Joseph. Meanwhile, perhaps Joseph assumed Jesus was traveling with Mary. Miles from Jerusalem they looked for Jesus but could not find him (Luke 2:44).

So why had Jesus remained behind at the Temple in Jerusalem? This was not a teenager experimenting with independence but rather a purposeful delay meant to send a message. For the first time in Luke's Gospel and the only time before Jesus's baptism, we hear him speak: "Why were you searching for me? . . . Didn't you know I had to be in my Father's house?" (Luke 2:49). In this statement, Jesus himself proclaimed his identity and purpose.

This specific time when Jesus traveled to Jerusalem was different from others. Messianic expectation was particularly high because it was Passover, which reminded the Jewish pilgrims of God's deliverance from Egyptian bondage. Also, the seventy-year cycle of Jewish nationalism had arrived. Earlier in Israel's history the Lord God had promised and provided deliverance after seventy years of Babylonian exile (Jer. 25:11–12).[44]

At the time of the Gospels, Jerusalem and its Temple had again become subject to foreign rule as the Romans took over in 63 BC. Thus seventy years later (AD 7) when Jesus was in the twelfth year of his earthly life, thoughtful Hebrews were looking for a deliverer to bring in God's Kingdom and restore true worship in the Temple (2 Sam. 7:13).[45] At just that moment, we find Jesus in the Temple where he needed to be about his Father's business, initiating God's plan of rescue and restoration.

◄ The walled area of Jerusalem encompasses some of ancient Jerusalem, where Jesus remained when he was twelve years old.

A young man celebrating his Bar Mitzvah at the western wall.

PART 2

JESUS REVEALS HIS LEGITIMATE AUTHORITY

Mount of Temptation (Quarantal).

During the first century, the land promised to Abraham was filled with Roman soldiers who had taken possession of the country by force. An extension of that Roman power lay in the hands of the Roman-appointed priestly aristocracy who had taken control of Jerusalem's Temple. They had used their wealth and political influence to obtain and maintain their fraudulent authority over the Temple institution. In the midst of these claims of authority, there was Jesus.

All authority in heaven and on earth actually belonged to him (Dan. 7:13–14; Matt. 28:18). In contrast to others, his was the legitimate authority. From place to place he revealed his authority through his words and actions that resulted in the overthrow of evil. In part 2 we will look at various ways Jesus revealed his authority and see again how certain places were often part of that process. In these eleven chapters we will examine events that occurred in places including the Judean Wilderness, the southern Jordan River valley, Nazareth, and the environs of Capernaum.

The Judean Wilderness and southern Jordan River valley were the location for the ministry of John the Baptist, whose coming was prophesied by Isaiah (40:3). We will see that this region provided John with a venue far from the corrupt Temple leadership and a setting that fulfilled the prophecies about him. Jesus came to John to be baptized in the Jordan River along the edge of the Judean Wilderness. We will consider why baptism in that river and in that region was appropriate to announce Jesus's authority as a rabbi and reveal him as Messiah.

After his baptism, the Wilderness of Judea became the place where the Spirit of God led Jesus. There in that desolate wilderness, Jesus initially revealed his authority over Satan. The adversary tempted Jesus to circumvent God's plan for rescue, and we will discuss the nature of the temptations as they pertained to Jesus's earthly needs, divine purpose, and political authority.

Nazareth was the place where Jesus revealed his assigned purpose to the community in which he grew up. In the synagogue in Nazareth Jesus pronounced his messianic authority with a strong rebuke for their rejection of God's rescuing power.

The bulk of part 2 finds us in and around Capernaum, where Jesus moved to fulfill a prophecy made about Capernaum in light of its past. But that is just the beginning. It was along the shore of the Sea of Galilee at Capernaum that he called disciples to become fishers of men. He cast out an evil spirit in the synagogue on the Sabbath. He declared a disabled man's sins forgiven in a private home. He pointed out and responded to the strong faith of a Roman. He even paid the annual Temple tax, albeit in an unexpected way. In each of these accounts and in each of these locations, Capernaum is a key to understanding the message of Jesus's legitimate rabbinic and messianic authority.

Capernaum excavations (view looking southwest).　　Pool used for ritual purification (Hebrew, *mikveh*).　　*Tilapia galilea*—St. Peter's Fish.

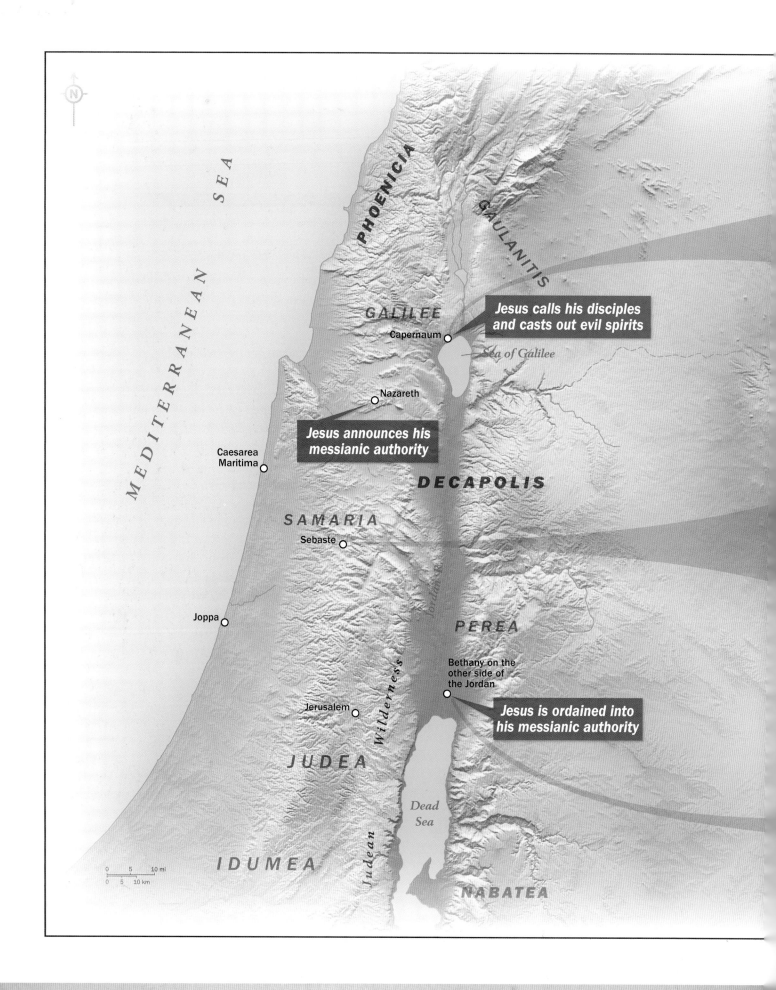

SEA

MEDITERRANEAN

PHOENICIA

GAULANITIS

GALILEE

Capernaum

Jesus calls his disciples
and casts out evil spirits

Sea of Galilee

Nazareth

Jesus announces his
messianic authority

Caesarea
Maritima

DECAPOLIS

SAMARIA

Sebaste

Joppa

PEREA

Bethany on the
other side of
the Jordan

Jerusalem

Jesus is ordained into
his messianic authority

Jordan

Wilderness

JUDEA

Dead
Sea

Judean

0   5   10 mi
0   5   10 km

IDUMEA

NABATEA

Capernaum
(view looking
northeast).

Forum at Samaria
(Sebaste).

Jordan River near
Bethany on the
other side of
the Jordan (view
looking south).

JOHN THE BAPTIST PREACHES IN THE WILDERNESS

MATTHEW 3:1–12

John the Baptist was sent to prepare the way for the coming of the Messiah. We might expect to see this important advance work unfolding in the capital city of Jerusalem. Instead, just as was prophesied, John preached, taught, and made disciples in the remote landscape of the Judean Wilderness (Isa. 40:3; Mal. 3:1; Matt. 3:1–3). And he did so for a reason.

John's father, Zechariah, was serving as a priest in the Temple when an angel of the Lord told him what to name his son, that his son would be filled with the Holy Spirit even from birth, and what his son's assignment would be (Luke 1:8–22). Though unable to speak because of his disbelief, Zechariah later rejoiced when his tongue was loosed after the birth of John. He was filled with the Holy Spirit and said, "And you, my child, . . . will go on before the Lord to prepare the way for him," which confirmed specifically what Isaiah and Malachi had prophesied (Luke 1:76; see also Luke 1:67–80; 3:2–6).

Like his father, John was a priest.[1] As a descendant of the priestly family, we would expect John to serve at the Temple from time to time (Luke 1:5). Whether or not he ever served in the Temple, the Gospels record that he preached and taught in the wilderness far from the Temple complex for two important reasons.

First, in the second century BC the Greek king Antiochus IV had imposed Greek culture and religion on his subjects. He deposed the legitimate high priestly family of Zadok, who had led Israelite worship in Jerusalem since the time of David and Solomon. In their place he appointed illegitimate high priests who promised to provide him significant income and who were willing to support his efforts to Hellenize Jerusalem.[2]

Things had not changed much by the time the Romans arrived in 63 BC, only now it was the Roman, not Greek, government that had appointed a fraudulent high priestly aristocracy to control the Temple. These aristocratic families continued to misuse their powerful positions in the Temple for personal gain. Their self-serving actions resulted in many warnings of the disaster that would one day come upon them (Matt. 24:15–16; Mark 13:2, 14; Luke 19:41–47; see also Dan. 9:26–27; 11:31–32; 12:11).

John the Baptist disassociated himself from a corrupt priesthood. Living in the Judean Wilderness, John ate locusts and wild honey provided by the Lord.

This statuette of John the Baptist portrays him wearing clothes, possibly a woven garment, made of camel's hair (Matt. 3:4).

Bethany on the other side of the Jordan. ▶
John the Baptist baptized in the Jordan Valley in this region.

Following the example of the prophet Elijah, John wore garments woven of camel hair with a leather belt around his waist (Matt. 3:4; Mark 1:6).[3] Dressed in the prophetic authority of Elijah (Matt. 11:7–14), John baptized at the Jordan River those who confessed their sins (Matt. 3:5–6). In the wilderness, away from corrupt or censoring troublemakers back at the Temple complex, John spread the good news of the coming Messiah (Luke 3:18).

The second reason for John's presence in the wilderness was connected to Isaiah 40:3 and Malachi 3:1. Hundreds of years earlier, these two men had prophesied of an individual who would prepare the way "in the desert" for the coming of the Messiah. In the wilderness, John fulfilled the prophecies of Isaiah and Malachi. John's message that prepared the way of the Lord also put Jerusalem's corrupt priesthood on notice. The Messiah was about to arrive and bring true worship into the Temple (2 Sam. 7:13).

The Judean Wilderness

Grasshopper (locust) laying eggs in the Judean Wilderness.

JESUS IS BAPTIZED IN THE LIVING WATER OF THE JORDAN RIVER

MATTHEW 3:13–15

The Gospel writers point us to any number of watershed moments in the life of Jesus—moments that dramatically changed his life on earth. But the first such moment is one that literally involved water. From the day of his baptism, Jesus was recognized as one who taught with authority, and he was baptized in the water of the Jordan River for a reason.

Within the culture of first-century Judaism, ritual immersion in water was used in a variety of ways, each of which involved *living* water. The Jewish oral law known as the Mishnah carefully defines various sources for such living water. The purest form of living water is rainfall. Therefore, any water source that flows or directs rainfall is said to contain living water.[4] Thus by definition, the water of a river, lake, or sea was considered living water. A manmade pool (Hebrew, *mikveh*) could also contain living water if it was constructed properly and was fed from a source that collected and directed water to that pool.[5]

Such natural or manmade receptacles for living water were employed in various Jewish rituals,[6] the most common being ritual purification. Various actions, experiences, and even certain bodily secretions could make one ritually unclean. Jewish law provided the definition of such impurity and charted the path to ritual cleanness, one of which was ritual immersion in living water.

But when Jesus requested that John baptize him, he was not seeking ritual purification; rather, Jesus used baptism to mark his entrance into public office (see Num. 8:5–7; 1 Kings 1:38–40). Jesus had reached the age of thirty (Luke 3:23), and it is no coincidence that he sought baptism from John at this time because it marked the moment within Jewish society when one reached the age of authority.[7]

Why did he choose to use the water of the Jordan River? First of all, not just any water would do; the water used for this baptism had to be living water. Because the Jordan River naturally collected rainwater and directed it downstream, it fit the definition within Jewish law of living water.

If we go back in history, we find another association with the living water of the Jordan. At the time of Moses, the Promised Land included territory

Painting (AD 1455) of Jesus coming to the Jordan River to be baptized by John the Baptist.

Jesus's Baptism at Bethany
on the Other Side of the Jordan

Jordan River near Bethany on the other
side of the Jordan, where Jesus was baptized.

just east of the Jordan River (Deut. 3:17).[8] When the Lord opened the waters of the flooding Jordan River allowing Joshua and the Israelites access to the Promised Land (Josh. 3:14–17), the river became synonymous with fulfillment of his promises. A monument had been built by the river to remind Israelites of the miraculous crossing of the Jordan and to highlight the reliability of God's word (Josh. 4:19–24). No promise loomed larger in Scripture than God's promise to provide the coming Rescuer. Thus when Jesus was inaugurated into his role as the Messiah, he chose to be baptized with the living water of the Jordan River—a water source that not only fit the definition of living water but also was a place long associated with the reminder that God keeps his promises.

Sarcophagus frieze (fourth century) depicting the baptism of Jesus.

JESUS BECOMES A RABBI IN THE SOUTHERN JORDAN VALLEY

MATTHEW 3:16–17

When Jesus's disciples spoke with him, they often addressed him as Rabbi (e.g., Matt. 26:25; Mark 9:5; 11:21; John 1:38, 49), a title he came to possess on the day of his baptism. Whatever else changed for Jesus on that day, this was the day he was ordained as a rabbi. We will see why that title was important to the work of Jesus and what message the setting of Jesus's baptism adds to that day.

During the early part of the first century, the title *rabbi* was undergoing a transition.[9] It had been used as an honorary title given to wise Jewish teachers. By the time Jesus was called Rabbi, the title conferred something similar to an academic degree on a student who had progressed sufficiently during several years of study under a scribe who had already demonstrated mastery of traditional Jewish interpretation. Thus, unlike the priesthood, it was not a person's family heritage but his scriptural understanding that made him eligible for this honor. The common people looked to their rabbi to provide authoritative and binding meaning of the Scriptures, as blind Bartimaeus submitted to Jesus as his rabbi (Mark 10:51).

Although at that time the authority to speak on the Scriptures was only recognized after approval was given by a senior rabbi,[10] Jesus brought his complete understanding of the Scriptures from God himself. The training and ordination of the Messiah was not limited to the ideas and traditions that had been developed by other rabbis. Nor was it a man limited with his own

Mt. Nebo (view looking east from Bethany on the other side of the Jordan), where Balaam prophesied the coming of the Messiah (Num. 24:17).

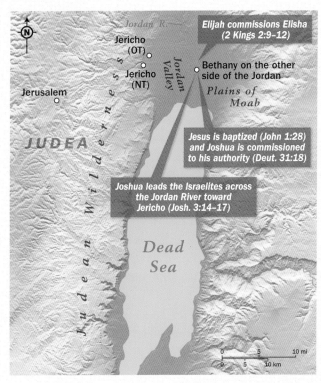

Jesus's Baptism at Bethany on the Other Side of the Jordan

opinions who pronounced Jesus worthy of his title of authority. Rather, heaven opened, the Spirit of God descended like a dove on Jesus, and the sky filled with the voice of the heavenly Father announcing his approval (Isa. 11:2–3; Matt. 3:17). This ordination of a rabbi was distinctly different from any other ordination because it declared Jesus to be the Messiah, the Rabbi of all rabbis.

It was not only the fact that this happened with Jesus's baptism but where it happened that merits our attention. Since John was baptizing at Bethany on the other side of the Jordan (John 1:28), we connect Jesus's baptism to the southern Jordan River valley.[11] This was the setting for an important prophecy about the Messiah that came from an unlikely source. During the days of Moses, the Israelites encamped on the plains of Moab just northeast of the Dead Sea. This so terrified the Moabites that they hired Balaam, a man well known for the practice of divination, to curse the Israelites. But Balaam was no match for the Lord, who influenced Balaam so that all he could do was bless the Israelites. On his fourth attempt to curse Israel, Balaam spoke of a special child of Jacob. "I see him, but not now; I behold him, but not near. A star will come out of Jacob;

a scepter will rise out of Israel" (Num. 24:17). What the Lord had spoken through Balaam was now being fulfilled at Bethany beyond the Jordan with the baptism of Jesus. So it was that Jesus came to be recognized as a rabbi and Messiah in order that the people of Israel might regard his words as having divine authority. And so it was that Jesus was publicly proclaimed rabbi and Messiah in this place where the promise of his coming had been proclaimed.

◄ The church at Bethany on the other side of the Jordan, denoting the consecration of Jesus into his rabbinic authority.

This Deir Alla inscription (eighth century BC) makes reference to curses pronounced by Balaam.

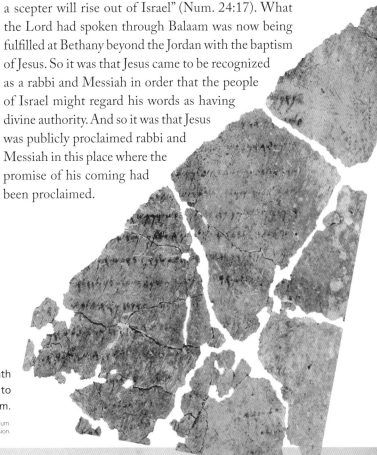

THE SPIRIT LEADS JESUS INTO THE WILDERNESS

MATTHEW 4:1–4

Jesus had barely emerged from the Jordan River, ordained by John the Baptist into his rabbinic and messianic authority, when the adversary entered to derail his mission. The Messiah would be tempted in every way that humans can be tempted, but he did not sin (Heb. 4:15). It is in this connection that Jesus was led by the Spirit of God into the Wilderness of Judea.

On the day of Jesus's baptism, the Spirit of God descended like a dove and remained on him (Matt. 3:16). Shortly after, the Holy Spirit led Jesus past the banks of the Jordan River and deep into the seclusion of the Judean Wilderness. There the barren beauty of this chalky wilderness is coupled with its stark desolation. This wilderness lacks the natural resources that invite sustained residence; nevertheless, Jesus remained there, fasting for forty days and forty nights.[12] As Jesus became hungry, Satan attempted to exploit the circumstances. He urged Jesus to prove himself to be the Son of God by turning stones into bread (Matt. 4:2–3).

The details associated with this temptation by Satan remind us of the experience of ancient Israel as summarized in Deuteronomy 8:2–3. In that account, following an extended stay in Egypt, the Lord delivered the children of Israel, bringing them toward the Promised Land by leading them through the wildernesses of Shur, Sin, Paran, and Zin (see Exod. 15:22; 16:1; Num. 10:12; 20:1). For both Jesus and the children of Israel the *wilderness* became the environment in which difficulties were encountered. For example, ancient Israel lacked food in the wilderness and therefore concluded that God had brought them into the wilderness to kill them. Consequently, he provided them with a daily supply of manna that became a staple of their diet until they entered the Promised Land (Exod. 16:3–4; Josh. 5:12). According to Moses, the Lord did so in order to teach the Israelites that "man does not live on bread alone but on every word that comes from the mouth of the Lord" (Deut. 8:2–3).

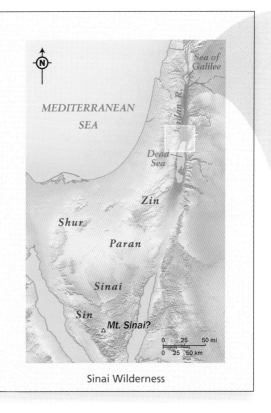

Sinai Wilderness

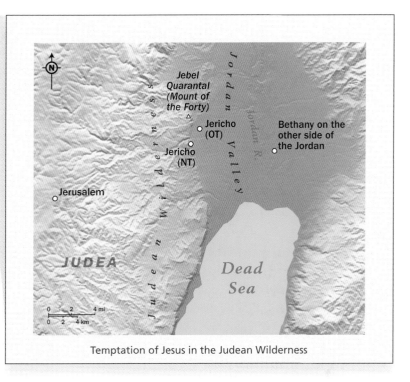

Temptation of Jesus in the Judean Wilderness

So it was that after his baptism into his rabbinic and messianic authority as the Son of God, Jesus was led by God's Spirit into the wilderness to fast for forty days. Similar to the earlier wilderness experiences of the Israelites, it might appear that the Lord brought Jesus into the wilderness to kill him. As the author of lies, murder, theft, and destruction (Gen. 3:1–4; John 8:44), certainly Satan wished that to be the case. But unlike the Israelites who blamed God for leading them into the stark and barren wilderness with its lack of food, Jesus saw the bigger picture. The Israelites who did not believe the Lord was their provider were focused on their immediate circumstances. Knowing that his Father is the provider for all of life in the midst of any circumstance, Jesus's focus was on representing God accurately. Thus, when confronted by Satan's temptation in the wilderness to prove he was the Son of God by turning the stones into bread, Jesus responded with God's perspective by quoting the words of Moses: "Man does not live on bread alone but on every word that comes from the mouth of the LORD" (Deut. 8:3; Matt. 4:4).

◀ Judean Wilderness. After his baptism by John the Baptist, Jesus was led into the Judean Wilderness by the Holy Spirit, where he was then tempted by the adversary.

Tempera-on-panel painting (AD 1455–60) by Giovanni di Paolo, depicting Jesus being led into the wilderness.

ANNOUNCEMENT IN THE SYNAGOGUE AT NAZARETH

LUKE 4:14–30

Following Jesus's forty days in the wilderness where he was tempted by Satan to prove himself to be the Son of God, he returned to the Galilee where he taught in that region's synagogues (Luke 4:14–15). On one Sabbath Jesus entered the synagogue in Nazareth in which they followed an order that included a public reading from the Prophets. When it came time for that reading, Jesus stood up and was handed a scroll of the book of Isaiah from which he was expected to read (Luke 4:17).

Unrolling the scroll to the verses of Isaiah 61 that announce the coming of the Messiah, Jesus read, "The Spirit of the Lord is on me, because he has anointed me to preach good news to the poor" (Luke 4:18; see Isa. 61:1). Then Jesus rolled up the scroll, gave it back to the attendant, and sat down. It was the custom of the day for the reader to also give a sermon and for rabbis to sit when they taught, and Jesus did exactly that.[13] Perhaps he sat in the chair called the Seat of Moses (Matt. 23:2), which was provided in synagogues for that purpose.[14] A rabbi teaching from this seat was considered to be making an announcement that had binding authority on his listeners. Jesus announced to those present, "Today this scripture is fulfilled in your hearing" (Luke 4:21).

Luke had already recorded a series of announcements regarding the coming of the Messiah:

The angel Gabriel announced to Zechariah that his son, John, would "make ready a people prepared for the Lord" (Luke 1:17).

Biram Synagogue from Galilee. No remains from the first-century synagogue of Nazareth in Galilee have been discovered, but it may have been similar in size to this synagogue.

With the birth of his son, Zechariah prophesied that John would "go on before the Lord to prepare the way for him" (Luke 1:76).

Gabriel announced to Mary in Nazareth that she would be the mother of the Son of God (Luke 1:32, 35).

Seat of Moses in the Israel Museum. The seat of Moses was located in the synagogue, where rabbis could proclaim authoritative statements.

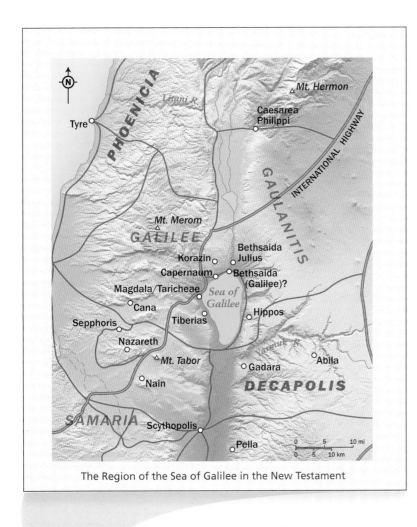

The Region of the Sea of Galilee in the New Testament

When Mary greeted Elizabeth, even the baby in Elizabeth's womb leaped for joy (Luke 1:44).

Elizabeth announced that Mary was "the mother of [my] Lord" (Luke 1:43).

To the shepherds, the angelic host heralded Jesus's birth as the arrival of the Messiah (Luke 2:11).

When the baby Jesus was taken to the Temple, Simeon and Anna announced that he was God's Anointed One (Luke 2:25–38).

John the Baptist, who was "a voice of one calling in the desert," announced, "Prepare the way for the Lord" (Luke 3:4).

Jesus returned to the place where his mother had been told of his coming, where Mary and Joseph had shown their courage and faith in God, and where people were the most likely to question his birth and mistakenly condemn Mary and Joseph for what they thought was adultery. Thus it is no coincidence that Jesus proclaimed in Nazareth's synagogue that he was the Messiah, the fulfillment of all the messianic promises proclaimed by the prophets.

The Nazareth Ridge as seen from Mt. Tabor. The city of Nazareth was located on this ridge.

Division of Herod the Great's Kingdom

Antipas
Philip
Procuratorship
Syrian

JESUS MOVES TO CAPERNAUM

MATTHEW 4:12–17

The baptism of Jesus and his defeat of Satan's temptations were both acts that revealed his legitimate authority. They occurred in the regions of Perea and Judea, but soon after, Jesus went back to the Galilee where he established a more permanent residence in Capernaum. For the next few years, this village was known as "his own town" (Matt. 9:1). We will see that Jesus relocated to Capernaum for a reason.

Matthew offers an explanation for this move: Jesus left Nazareth in the area of Zebulun to live by the Sea of Galilee in the area of Naphtali in order to fulfill what was said through the prophet Isaiah (Matt. 4:13–16). To draw attention to the fact that Jesus's relocation to Capernaum fulfilled prophecy, Matthew even quotes a portion of Isaiah 9 that speaks about a light dawning in the dark regions of Zebulun and Naphtali in the Galilee of the Gentiles (Isa. 9:1–2; 42:6–7).

If we explore the history of this region and the larger message of Isaiah 9, it will become clear why Capernaum was selected for this particular honor. The history of Zebulun and Naphtali is filled with horrible times of foreign occupation. Since the Promised Land is a land bridge connecting the continents of Asia, Africa, and Europe, it frequently was the target of foreign invasion by those wishing to cash in on the trade and tax revenues this land promised, and Naphtali and Zebulun faced the brunt of the occupations. Among the earliest of those invasions was that of the Assyrians, which had been prophesied in the eighth century BC. At that time the Lord had spoken to his people through the prophet Isaiah, warning of the time when the Assyrians would attack and ravage the land (Isaiah 8). It was Zebulun and Naphtali in particular that absorbed the ravages of the Assyrian king (2 Kings 15:29).

In the first century BC the Romans brought violence and hardship to the people living near Capernaum. Herod the Great was attempting to solidify the Roman control in this region, which was known as the "Galilee of the Gentiles" (Matt. 4:15). Toward that end, he

Arbel cliffs and plain of Magdala (view looking northeast toward Capernaum).

sought to clean out the resistance fighters who had hidden themselves and their families in cave homes lining the steep cliffs above the Valley of the Pigeons near Arbela, just west of Capernaum. Those resisting Rome thought the topography of the region would provide adequate protection. But Herod had Roman soldiers lowered in baskets over the edge of the cliff to slaughter the families.[15] These are but two examples of the way Zebulun and Naphtali felt the weight of foreign occupation.[16]

If there was a dark place that needed the light of hope, this was it. That is why God promised this region that it would receive the Messiah's special attention. Those living in the shadow of death and darkness of Gentile occupation would enjoy the dawning of the light (Isa. 9:2). Upon the birth of a special child, things would change dramatically. The warrior's boots and bloody garments of war would be discarded and used as fuel for the fire (Isa. 9:5). For that special child would be the Messiah who would inherit the throne of David, the government would be on his shoulders, and foreign occupiers would be defeated as he established an eternal Kingdom. He would be called "Wonderful Counselor, Mighty God, Everlasting Father, Prince of Peace" (Isa. 9:6; see vv. 1–7).

Aerial view of Capernaum looking southwest toward Magdala and the Arbel cliffs.

As Israel looked forward to this day of liberation, Jesus moved to Capernaum, which was ideally situated along the way of the sea, in order to fulfill Isaiah's prophecy (Isa 9:1–2; Matt. 4:13–15). Jesus moved to this place to proclaim a message of rescue: the one who brought the Kingdom of God had come to give life to a world of death.

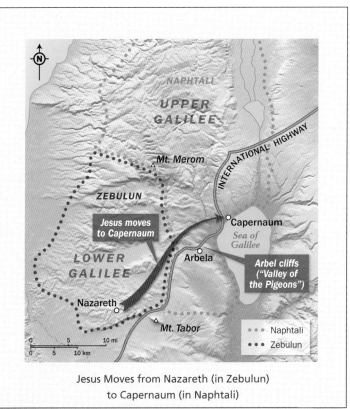

Jesus Moves from Nazareth (in Zebulun) to Capernaum (in Naphtali)

Mile marker denoting the Via Maris (international highway), which passed through Capernaum.

CATCHING MEN
AT THE SEA OF GALILEE

LUKE 5:1–11

As Jesus taught by the Sea of Galilee, the crowds grew so large that some of the people were unable to hear him. So Jesus got into Simon's fishing boat and asked him to push off a short distance from the shore. This allowed his voice to be amplified by the natural amphitheater formed by the hills sloping up from the lakeshore. It also allowed Jesus to teach his disciples aspects of "fishing" from God's perspective.

The boat Jesus used belonged to Simon, who had been fishing all night with his partners James and John. The clues in Luke's account help us picture the kind of fishing they were doing. The combination of washing nets, deep water, and night (Luke 5:2, 4–5) suggest that these men were using trammel nets, which are hung upright in the water like a wall. "Unlike other nets that have only one 'wall,' this is a compound net consisting of three layers held together by a single corked head rope and a

Fishermen mending trammel nets (ca. AD 1900).

single leaded foot rope."[17] The three layers were carefully designed to entangle the fish between them. This technique was particularly effective when it was used in the deeper waters of the lake and at night when the fish were unable to see the net. Once the night of fishing was done, the silt was washed from the nets on shore.[18]

When Jesus directed him to take his boat, net, and partners back on to the lake, Simon objected. They had worked hard all night and had caught nothing (Luke 5:4–5). But they did return to the lake, and their net filled with so many fish that they had to signal for another boat to come and help with the catch. Both boats were so filled with fish that they began to sink. The miracle had its desired effect on Simon, James, and John. Just as Jesus caught them at the Sea of Galilee, so his message and this miracle persuaded them to leave everything and follow him to "catch men" (Luke 5:11).

The fact that Jesus declared that Simon, James, and John would catch men further illustrates the great impact these men would have as Jesus's disciples. If while

Cast-net fishing at sunset on the Sea of Galilee.

catching fish under Jesus's direction these disciples could find such great success, we can better comprehend what occurred later as they began to catch men. When the day of Pentecost came, Peter spoke, and thousands came to know Jesus in just one day (Acts 2:41). As those who believed met day after day in the Temple, united in purpose, the Lord kept adding to their number daily (Acts 2:46–47). James (considered the brother of Jesus) led believers in Jerusalem. And John, who led believers in Asia Minor, provided biblical writings, including a Gospel record, letters, and the book of Revelation, that have been used to catch people for two thousand years. Thus Jesus's words to these disciples were fulfilled in ways they could never have imagined.

Fishermen on the Sea of Galilee.

Capernaum fishing cove (view looking southeast).

EVIL SPIRIT IN THE SYNAGOGUE AT CAPERNAUM

MARK 1:21–28

Capernaum is located on the northwest shore of the Sea of Galilee. That meant something significant to people living in the first century who saw that its area around the Sea of Galilee and loyalty to God had something in common.[19] Those living on the southeast side of the Sea of Galilee in the region known as the Decapolis were at one end of the loyalty spectrum. The Decapolis was Gentile country and focused on Greco-Roman idolatry. It was also where one would expect to find pork for dinner and people possessed by demons (Matt. 8:28–34; Mark 5:1–20).

By contrast, the northwest side of the lake was in the region known as Galilee and had a significant population of observant and Hellenized Jews. The villages in the more observant regions of Galilee included Capernaum, Korazin, and Bethsaida. These villages were particularly religious areas where people followed Jewish dietary laws, studied the Scriptures, and attempted to avoid the idolatry that was particularly rampant on the lake's other side.

Surprisingly, it was in the context of this religious environment that evil spirits had come to Capernaum—a city given special status by Jesus. Matthew tells us that Jesus moved there from Nazareth to live in fulfillment of Isaiah's prophecy (Matt. 4:12–16; see Isa. 9:1–7). It is called both his "home" (Mark 2:1) and "his own town" (Matt. 9:1). If demons came to the northwest side of the lake, we at least expect them to avoid Capernaum. They did not.

A confrontation between Jesus and an evil spirit occurred not just in Capernaum but in the synagogue and on the Sabbath. The Jews of Capernaum had built their synagogue as a place consecrated to God[20]—the place to hear his Scriptures, worship, and pray.[21] Therefore, how disgraceful was the presence of an evil spirit in this sacred space, particularly when it occurred on the Sabbath, the day which God had claimed as his own (Exod. 20:8–11).

Stone head of the Babylonian demon Pazuzu (800–500 BC).

This terra-cotta demon mask from Ur dates to the time of Abraham and the patriarchs (2,000–1,700 BC).

Basalt foundation of Capernaum's first-century synagogue, where Jesus did numerous miracles, including casting out demons.

This demon in the synagogue in Capernaum on the Sabbath displayed an arrogance of the highest degree as well as a high level of aggression—it did not wait for Jesus to come over to the other side of the lake (Decapolis) but instead challenged the authority of Jesus right in the synagogue of his own town. But the evil spirit's arrogance and aggression was no match for Jesus, who responded with authority, "Be quiet! . . . Come out of him!" (Mark 1:25). Those words completely thwarted the demon, forcing it to obey. And so it was that Jesus proclaimed the Kingdom of God and reclaimed the world from the adversary—one region, one city, one synagogue, and even one person at a time.

Reconstruction of Capernaum's first-century synagogue.

AUTHORITY TO FORGIVE SINS ON EARTH

LUKE 5:17–25

Within a short period of time Jesus became a very popular rabbi. Pharisees and teachers of the law walked to Capernaum from Galilee, Judea, and even Jerusalem to determine if Jesus's authority was legitimate (Luke 5:17, 21). While Jesus was in a home discussing Scripture with these religious leaders, a paralyzed man was carried there by his friends. The disabled man was brought for healing; the Jewish teachers had come to determine if Jesus was teaching with legitimate authority. Here we will see why both groups traveled to meet Jesus and why this setting was used to reveal his authority to forgive sins.

Because the crowd blocked the entrance, the paralytic man was lowered through the roof in order to get to Jesus. Jesus said to the man, "Friend, your sins are forgiven" (Luke 5:20). For the Jewish teachers, this pronouncement raised the question of the extent of Jesus's authority because this declaration was one only God could make (Luke 5:21). According to their understanding, rabbis not only taught with authority, but some were even seen as having authority to do miracles.[22] But no rabbi before or after Jesus thought it within their authority to forgive sins. Thus in this situation Jesus was clearly stating that his authority to forgive sins was directly from God and part of his messianic mission.

Saying, "But that you may know that the Son of Man has authority on earth to forgive sins," Jesus directed the man to pick up his mat and go home (Luke 5:25).[23] Thus in word and deed Jesus demonstrated that he carried a level of authority that far exceeded that of any rabbi (Matt. 23:8–10).

While in Capernaum, Jesus was teaching, preaching, and healing many, including Simon Peter's mother-in-law (Mark 1:29–34; 2:2–12; Luke 4:38–41).[24] This in

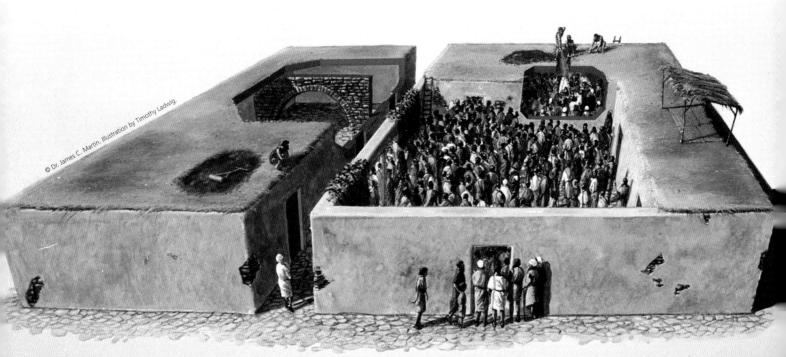

Illustration of Jesus healing the paralytic at Capernaum.

turn explains why both the disabled man and the Jewish teachers had gone to Capernaum, because it was there Jesus was teaching and doing miracles.[25] The question was, did the ability to do miracles prove the miracle worker was from God? Jesus answered the question not only by doing miracles but by forgiving sins, which was for God alone to do.

Later, while meeting with his eleven apostles, the resurrected Jesus declared, "All authority in heaven and earth has been given to me" (Matt. 28:18). The demons had recognized Jesus. At Capernaum an intrusive evil spirit said, "I know who you are—the Holy One of God!" (Mark 1:24).

With the miracle in Capernaum, Jesus revealed the far-reaching nature of his authority by healing the paralytic and declaring the forgiveness of sins. It is important to observe that the location for this event was not the Temple in Jerusalem or even a synagogue—both traditional Jewish strongholds of religious authority. Instead Jesus demonstrated that the authority of the Messiah to heal and to forgive sins extends into every public and private sphere on earth—even a private home. So it was that the Pharisees and the disabled man had come to this home, and so it was that Jesus used this home to make known his authority on earth.

Sarcophagus relief (fourth century) of the healing of the woman subject to bleeding.

Sarcophagus relief (fourth century) of Jesus healing the paralytic at the Bethesda Pools.

THE CENTURION'S FAITH IN CAPERNAUM

LUKE 7:1–10

Turn to any page in the Gospels and you are more likely to see Jesus teaching sons of Abraham than Gentiles. He had established his home in Capernaum, which was in the middle of an observant Jewish region[26] whose people considered the power of Rome and what it represented to be an extension of the kingdom of evil. Thus it would have appeared strange for Jesus to have a favorable interaction with a Roman military officer. But this centurion[27] in Capernaum loved the nation of Israel and had the affection of the local Jewish community leaders. He had even built Capernaum's synagogue (Luke 7:4–5). We do not know his name, but we do know his title and consequently that he was a Gentile.

As Jesus entered the city, a delegation of Jewish leaders approached bringing a request for him to help the Roman centurion whose valued servant was critically ill. A centurion was a military officer who had command of a unit that in the period of the Gospels could number up to one hundred men. Whether this officer had been appointed by Rome or by one of the provincial governors, he was a Gentile with significant power and authority. Therefore he could have forced Jesus to come, but instead he humbly sought help and completely submitted to

Relief of a Roman soldier guarding a captured Gaul.

Bronze Antoninianus coin, stamped with the standard of the Roman Legion.

Jesus's authority, believing he could heal his servant just by saying the word (Luke 7:7). Jesus not only granted the centurion's request but also celebrated his faith, noting that he had not discovered this kind of faith anywhere else in Israel (Luke 7:9).

All this happened in Capernaum for a reason. First of all, the setting explains why this city provided Jesus with an opportunity to interact with a Gentile centurion. At Capernaum, where topography narrowed and directed passage of international trade, the Romans were likely to have established a customs station. Thus, Roman soldiers would be quartered in the region to guarantee the security of that station.

Stamped tile of the Tenth Roman Legion.

The words Jesus spoke to this man take on added meaning in light of the setting, for Capernaum was a stronghold of observant Judaism, which generally viewed Gentiles as enemies to be eliminated.[28] They commonly held that the day of the Messiah's arrival would include a feast attended by the redeemed of Israel and the great leaders of Israel's past—a feast that excluded all Gentiles.[29] It was here at Capernaum that this preconception was being transformed.

In the parallel account in Matthew (Matt. 8:5–13), after celebrating the unique faith of this centurion, Jesus said, "I say to you that many will come from the east and the west, and will take their places at the feast with Abraham, Isaac and Jacob in the kingdom of heaven" (Matt. 8:11). Thus Capernaum not only provided the opportunity for Jesus to interact with such a Gentile, it also provided an observant Jewish setting in which Jesus could reveal that his authority and Kingdom extended more broadly than the Jewish community had thought.

Relief proclaiming Roman victory over Judea.

TEMPLE TAX COLLECTORS AND JESUS QUESTION PETER IN CAPERNAUM

MATTHEW 17:24–27

J esus and his disciples had just been in the region of Caesarea Philippi where Jesus proclaimed "that he must go to Jerusalem and suffer many things at the hands of the elders, chief priests and teachers of the law" (Matt. 16:21). Shortly after this proclamation they returned to Capernaum where Temple tax collectors from Jerusalem asked Peter, "Doesn't your teacher pay the temple tax?" (Matt. 17:24).

This annual Temple tax was collected in the spring of the year from Jewish males who had reached or exceeded the age of twenty, and Moses informed the people this money was to be used for the service of the Tent of Meeting (Exod. 30:14–16). By the eighth century BC the money was considered a tax levied for the Temple built by Solomon (2 Chron. 24:4–10). This practice continued through the Temple's history in order to support its daily operations, upkeep, and improvement.[30] So Jewish men, no matter where they might be living in the world, fulfilled their duty to the Jerusalem Temple by paying this annual tax.[31]

The question the Temple tax collectors asked Peter concerning whether Jesus paid the Temple tax appears to be motivated by Jesus's proclaimed authority over the Temple (Matt. 12:6).

Ancient fish hooks like these were used by Galilean fishermen.

What better way for the Temple vanguard to test this Galilean rabbi's teachings about the Jerusalem Temple than to confront one of Jesus's most qualified disciples on his own turf, Capernaum (Matt. 16:17–19). The fact that the disciples were well aware that Jesus was considered a great threat to the Jerusalem Temple leadership (Matt. 16:21) meant that Peter understood the gravity of the question levied by these Temple tax collectors.

The Latin name for St. Peter's Fish is *Tilapia galilea*. In Hebrew it is called *am nun*, which means "mother fish," because it cares for its young in its mouth.

for the two of them from resources provided by God. Peter went to the lake, threw in a fishing line, and took a coin for the exact amount of the Temple tax out of the mouth of the first fish he caught.[32] Various species of fish fill this lake, but one in particular inhabits the waters near Capernaum in the springtime. It is now called Saint Peter's Fish in memory of this event.[33]

After Peter affirmed that Jesus paid the Jerusalem Temple tax, he entered the house and Jesus asked him, "From whom do the kings of the earth collect duty and taxes—from their own sons or from others?" Peter responded, "From others," to which Jesus replied, "Then the sons are exempt" (Matt. 17:25–26).

As Messiah, Jesus confirmed both his authority over the Temple (2 Sam. 7:11–13) and his destiny to fulfill the symbolic sacrifices that occurred within it (Heb. 10:1–10). He was King of the Universe, including the Temple. Jesus brought in the Kingdom of God, and those who belonged to him also became exempt from paying the Temple tax.

In order to prevent the issue of the Temple tax from becoming an offense (Matt. 17:27), Jesus instructed Peter to pay the tax. Rather than taking money from the purse (see John 12:6), however, Jesus instructed Peter to pay the tax

Tyrian shekels such as these were required payment for the Temple tax.

© Dr. James C. Martin. The Eretz Israel Museum, Tel Aviv. Photographed by permission.

Tilapia galilea, known as St. Peter's Fish.

PART 3

JESUS'S PARABLES AND TEACHING

Agricultural watchtower.

Jesus drew large crowds to his side on a daily basis. His listeners "were amazed at his teaching, because his message had authority" (Luke 4:32). Jesus's instructions were also highly visual, illustrated by the places and objects that surrounded him. As Jesus taught his listeners profound and eternal truths, he turned their attention back to the places, tasks, and objects of everyday living. The goal of part 3 is to visit the highly visual and vibrant nature of Jesus's parables and teachings. We will see that he takes us to cities, grain fields, lakeshores, and sheepfolds for a reason.

Those who wish to fully gather all there is within Jesus's teachings will need to join his listeners in their physical and cultural settings. That is what we are going to do. In order to learn about the Kingdom of God, we will join those listeners in looking toward two cities, Magdala and Hippos—one associated with salt, the other with light. We will examine the road system in Israel in order to appreciate what it meant to walk a broad versus a narrow road. We will stand in a grain field with Jesus and hear his declaration that he is the Lord of the Sabbath. We will watch as a farmer sows seed and listen to Jesus speak of the uneven reception his message receives.

Then it is off to the shore of the Sea of Galilee where fishermen are removing the day's catch from their nets,

separating the good fish from the bad fish. Jesus then takes us into the open country where shepherds are grazing their flocks. Here we learn about a loving shepherd who leaves his vulnerable flock in order to recover an even more vulnerable lost sheep.

On the move again, this time we travel into a village home with a dirt floor in order to talk about the joy that accompanies finding a lost coin. As the sun sets, we go out again to the shepherds who bring their animals into the sheepfold for the night, and we see how those shepherds become the door of the shelter, limiting the access of those wishing to harm the flock.

Next we head for Jericho where we see a Jewish man beset and beaten by robbers. Here an unexpected act of kindness from a Samaritan illustrates whom we are to regard as our neighbor. In New Testament Jericho, the royal palace complex of Herod the Great comes into view. Jesus uses a parody that plays on the life of this king in order to outline the plan for his own life. Returning to the common setting of the house attached to the family living compound and to the vineyard, Jesus directs words of comfort to the disciples in advance of his impending crucifixion.

All these images were very familiar to Jesus's listeners. Part 3 will transport us to those locations so that we may see why Jesus taught in and about those places.

Wheat harvest.

Sheep looking out from the sheepfold.

Fishermen on the Sea of Galilee (early 1900s).

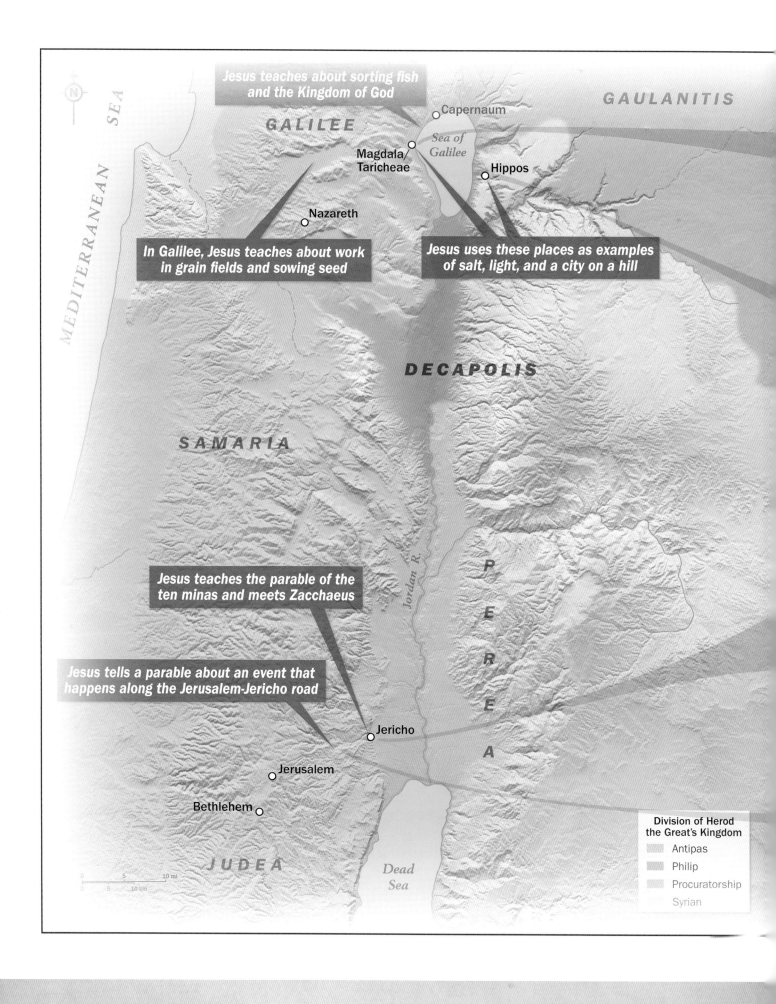

Jesus teaches about sorting fish
and the Kingdom of God

GAULANITIS

GALILEE

Capernaum

Sea of
Galilee

Magdala/
Taricheae

Hippos

Nazareth

In Galilee, Jesus teaches about work
in grain fields and sowing seed

Jesus uses these places as examples
of salt, light, and a city on a hill

DECAPOLIS

MEDITERRANEAN SEA

SAMARIA

Jordan R.

P
E
R
E
A

Jesus teaches the parable of the
ten minas and meets Zacchaeus

Jesus tells a parable about an event that
happens along the Jerusalem-Jericho road

Jericho

Jerusalem

Bethlehem

JUDEA

Dead
Sea

Division of Herod
the Great's Kingdom

Antipas

Philip

Procuratorship

Syrian

0   5   10 mi
0   5   10 km

Magdala/Taricheae at the base of the Arbel cliffs.

Decapolis city of Hippos (view looking north).

New Testament Jericho.

Remains of the first-century road from Jerusalem to Jericho.

SALT, LIGHT, AND A CITY ON A HILL

MATTHEW 5:13–16

Jesus's every intention was that the disciples whose lives he touched would have a positive effect on the lives of the people they touched. That is why he used this language when addressing them: "You are the salt of the earth. But if the salt loses its saltiness, how can it be made salty again? . . . You are the light of the world. A city on a hill cannot be hidden" (Matt. 5:13–14). We will see that he chose to use these metaphors where he did for a reason.

As Jesus taught throughout Galilee, large crowds came to hear him speak and to receive healing from their physical ailments (Matt. 4:23–25). On one occasion he spoke to the crowds on the hillside above the Sea of Galilee (Matt. 5:1; 7:28). He covered a wide range of topics in the extended discourse often called the Sermon on the Mount (Matthew 5–7), including salt, light, and a city on a hill.

While Jesus taught from this location, those gathered were familiar with both Magdala and Hippos—two important cities situated on the Sea of Galilee. Magdala was associated with salt and Hellenized

Lamp on lamp stand. Jesus used the imagery of lamp stands such as this one in his teachings on the importance of putting light in a place that removes as much darkness as possible.

Judaism.[1] Hippos was associated with Gentiles and was a city built on a hill. With these cities in mind, Jesus shaped his powerful lesson.

Magdala was on the northwestern plain of the Sea of Galilee. Fish harvested in that region of the lake were transported there to be processed with salt and then transported throughout the Roman Empire. So famous were these salted fish that came from Magdala that the Romans called the city Taricheae, which means "salted fish."[2]

Salt was an important and valuable commodity in New Testament times, which is why Jesus used the pertinent imagery of salt losing its value and being "no longer good for anything, except to be thrown out and trampled by men" (Matt. 5:13). The salt used in Magdala's fish processing was for the purpose of preservation; however, salt was also mixed with dung and used for fuel in ovens.[3] Once the salty dung mixture was burned, the salt residue lost its saltiness and no longer had any effect (Luke 14:34–35). So just as salt had an effect on

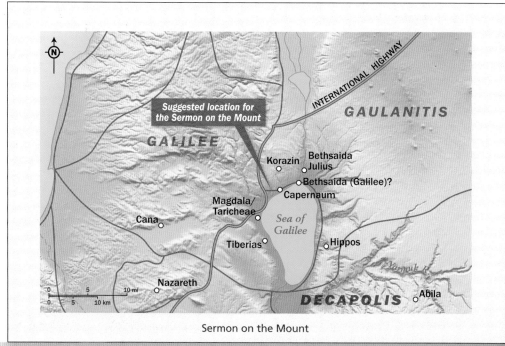

Sermon on the Mount

The Decapolis city of Hippos is situated on a hill on the east side of the Sea of Galilee, opposite Capernaum.

the fish and in the burning of dung fuel, so his followers were to have an effect on others.

The Gentile city of Hippos was located on a high hill above the east side of the Sea of Galilee. It was in fact a "city on a hill" that, like light, was not intended to be hidden (Matt. 5:14). The prominence of this city expressed Gentile superiority over the region with trade connected to Damascus.[4] As a Decapolis city, it was designed to propagate, influence, and direct Greco-Roman culture and ideology.

Probably speaking of Hippos in this metaphor, Jesus stated that his listeners were not to hide themselves any more than light is to be put under a bowl or a city on a hill is to be hidden. As his followers, they would not blend into the woodwork of society but were to be agents in affecting the world around them.

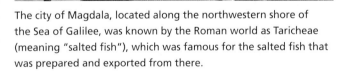

The city of Magdala, located along the northwestern shore of the Sea of Galilee, was known by the Roman world as Taricheae (meaning "salted fish"), which was famous for the salted fish that was prepared and exported from there.

Salt from the Dead Sea could be used in the salting of the fish from Taricheae (Magdala).

BROAD AND NARROW ROADS

MATTHEW 7:13–14

odern roads vary considerably from one to another. Six-lane freeways, two-lane state highways, and one-lane gravel roads each provide a different travel experience. The same was true in the world of the Bible. During the Sermon on the Mount, Jesus turned the attention of his listeners to roads in order to teach them about entering the Kingdom of God. Using an idiom that incorporated particular characteristics of Israel's geography, Jesus said, "Broad is the road that leads to destruction.... Narrow [is] the road that leads to life" (Matt. 7:13–14).

Travel patterns established the road system during the time of the Gospels. Whenever possible, people walked the shortest distance with the least change in elevation, so topography dictated travel routes in the Holy Land. As travelers and pack animals made repeated trips, a path was worn along the most desirable routes. For local journeys, a *road* was simply a well-worn path, sometimes just wide enough for those walking it.[5] The Romans, however, had created a complex road system that connected trade routes from Africa, Asia, and Europe that passed through the Promised Land.

Jesus's words had more to do with the terrain through which the road traveled than with the actual width of the road. The *broad* road to which Jesus referred may well have been the Romans' international highway that

coursed through open coastal plains and broad valleys of the Promised Land connecting Africa, Asia, and Europe. A section of this highway passing through the plain of Magdala was visible to Jesus and his listeners.

By contrast, the *narrow* roads were those in the interior of the country that made their way through the mountains by using narrow valleys through Samaria and ridges in Judea. Because the mountainous regions were more isolated than the coastal plains and their road systems more difficult to traverse, international traffic avoided these narrow roads. Thus the broad and narrow roads led through very different terrain and very different regions. The coastal plains and Galilee were geographical regions open and accessible to international travel and influence. Samaria was also relatively open, with valleys between the mountains that connected to the coast and Galilee. But access to Judea was restricted to the ridges and therefore more isolated.

Perhaps Jesus used that difference to teach about entering into the Kingdom of God. The *broad* road leading to destruction was like the international highway most frequently used by Gentiles passing through the Promised Land that became steeped in a pantheon of foreign idols and culture. Travel down that road may have been easier, but it was a road into assimilation that could lead the traveler away from the one true God.

The *narrow* roads were more difficult to travel due to the terrain through which they passed. But the more isolated the road, the less chance for assimilation into corrupting influences. "Broad is the road that leads to destruction. . . . Narrow [is] the road that leads to life" (Matt. 7:13–14).

Examples of Broad and Narrow Roads

International highway going along the Mediterranean coastline toward Egypt (view looking west).

◀ International highway going through the plain of Magdala (view looking northeast).

LORD OF THE SABBATH IN A GRAIN FIELD

LUKE 6:1–11

Judaism in the first century was pluralistic. Three sects described in the writings of the Jewish historian Josephus include Essenes, Sadducees, and Pharisees.[6] Essenes isolated themselves from the corruption of the world and fervently looked for the end of the age. The corrupt priesthood consisted of the Sadducees, who controlled the Temple in Jerusalem. Pharisees, including rabbis, scribes, and teachers of the law, ruled through the synagogues and were the most popular group among the common people.

In the first century, the world of the Pharisees was diverse and complex. The Jewish oral law, called the Mishnah, provides a great deal of information about the differences between two groups ("schools," or "houses") of Pharisees—the school of Shammai and the school of Hillel.[7] The teaching of Jesus in Galilee took place in the midst of escalating critical scrutiny from individuals in both schools of Pharisees, who vehemently

disagreed with his pronouncements on various points of Scripture.[8]

No rabbinic teaching in the Mishnah gets more detailed attention than observance of the Sabbath.[9] The Lord made it clear in the law that work was to be done on only six days of the week (Exod. 20:8–11). So important was the Sabbath that the Pharisees had made it their business to define in great detail what actions and activities constituted *work* and so were forbidden on this special day.[10]

There were thirty-nine classes of work that were not to be performed on the Sabbath; they included sowing, plowing, and reaping.[11] So it is not surprising that some Pharisees reprimanded Jesus when they saw his disciples picking, rubbing, and eating grain from the fields on the Sabbath (Luke 6:1–2). Pharisees believed work on the Sabbath was wrong and therefore subject to punishment. For some, profaning the Sabbath by

Woman harvesting grain in a wheat field.

© Direct Design.

Pharisees were in control of the synagogues such as this one at Gamla, which was in use during the time of the Gospels.

working was subject to a sin offering;[12] for others it was a capital offense that merited death by stoning.[13]

Jesus initially responded to the rebuke of the Pharisees by recalling an instance when the Sabbath was profaned by necessity: David ate the consecrated bread set aside for only the priest (1 Sam. 21:1–6). Then Jesus trumped even that precedent by revealing himself to be the Lord of the Sabbath (Luke 6:5). If anyone had a right to define what was and was not unlawful on that day, it was the one who had established it.

In the midst of this significant discussion, we almost forget that we are standing with all involved in a grain field. What does this setting add to the events transpiring before us? First of all, it suggests that the Pharisees have taken their surveillance of Jesus up a notch. We have become accustomed to seeing them scrutinizing Jesus in the synagogues or in the homes that regularly witnessed his ministry. But now they appear to be tracking his movements even on the Sabbath when he and the disciples happened to be walking through a grain field. Yet Jesus did not soften his language. In fact, if anything, the intensity of his pronouncement increased. There was no day of the week and there was no location in the land where he would not own his messianic identity and authority. That is why Jesus declared himself to be Lord of the Sabbath in a grain field.

◀ The Essenes believed they were the select "children of light" who would defeat the "children of darkness," as described in this Essene document known as the War Scroll.

© Dr. James C. Martin. Collection of the Israel Museum, Jerusalem, and courtesy of the Israel Antiquities Authority, exhibited at the Shrine of the Book, the Israel Museum, Jerusalem. Photographed by permission.

The Katros inscription. This inscribed stone was discovered in the Jerusalem estate of the Sadducean family of Katros.

© Dr. James C. Martin. The Wohl Archaeological Museum and Burnt House, Jerusalem.

SOWING SEED NEAR CAPERNAUM

MATTHEW 13:1–9

Due to the large crowd of followers, Jesus got into a boat and pushed off a short distance from the shoreline on the northwest side of the Sea of Galilee to teach about his Kingdom. At that particular moment the audience was receptive to him, but Jesus knew it would not be the case for long due to certain preconceptions the crowd had about the Messiah. So with words of warning and encouragement, he spoke to the crowd by using a parable that came from the immediate region.

Jesus turned the attention of his listeners to a very familiar scene—a farmer sowing his seed. As the seed tumbled through the air, it drifted onto various types of ground. Jesus interpreted the parable in this way: Seed that fell along the footpath and was eaten by birds was like God's Word that was proclaimed to people who heard it but did not understand, and it was then taken away from them by the evil one. The seed that fell in places where the topsoil only thinly covered the region's underlying basalt boulders illustrated those who quickly received God's message but wilted when trouble or persecution struck because their roots had not grown deep. The seed that fell among thorns sprouted but then gave way to the overgrowth of weeds. This illustrated those who initially received the message and then faded when worry or the deceit of wealth choked out any growth of God's Word in their life. But there were also those who received and retained God's Word. They were like

Thistles choke out the growth of grain.

Basaltic boulders in the region of Capernaum. Some of the basalt rocks lie just under the surface of the soil, allowing roots to grow only a few inches.

the good soil that received the seed and produced a phenomenal harvest (Matt. 13:18–23).

Jesus told this parable about a Galilean agricultural field for a reason. Galilee in general and the plains around the Sea of Galilee in particular were filled with agricultural fields.[14] Since 80 to 90 percent of the local residents were directly involved in agriculture,[15] Jesus's listeners not only understood the images but also knew that a good field would yield from ten to fifteen times what was planted. So when Jesus spoke about a harvest up to one hundred times what was sown (Matt. 13:23),[16] he was increasing the norm to

Plowing the ground is necessary to prepare for planting.

Road going through a ▶ Capernaum field.

make this point. His Kingdom would be filled with an exceptional number of people.

Yet even this large number of people did not mean everyone, and that was an issue to Jesus's audience on the northwest side of the Sea of Galilee. Recall that this side of the lake was populated with those dedicated to observant Judaism.[17] These Jews were eagerly awaiting the arrival of the promised Messiah. It could be assumed that upon his arrival many Jews would quickly welcome him and his message. Thus the message of this parable was specifically targeted in this place to correct that misperception. Jesus and his message would at first be acknowledged but then sometimes lost or even rejected. Rejection did not disqualify him from being the Messiah. Those who accepted and submitted to Jesus's authority were assured that they would be part of a bountiful harvest.

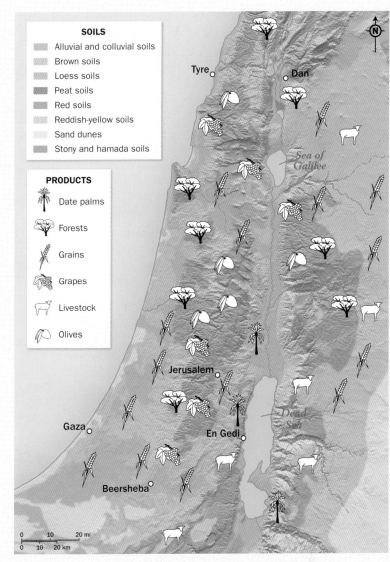

Agricultural Products of the Promised Land

SORTING FISH AND THE KINGDOM OF GOD

MATTHEW 13:47–50

Jesus had opened the day speaking to people from a fishing boat on the Sea of Galilee (Matt. 13:1–2); he closed the day in a house beside the Sea of Galilee speaking with his disciples about fishing. Jesus had called a number of these men while they were fishing and had redefined their life's work to be "fishers of men" (Matt. 4:19; see vv. 18–22). Now on the shore of that lake where they pursued their profession, Jesus used a parable to speak about the Kingdom of God using imagery with which they were familiar.

There are three general types of fishing nets that were used in the Sea of Galilee during the first century. The first is the *cast net*, which Peter and Andrew were using when Jesus called them to follow him (Matt. 4:18). James and his brother John were in a boat using the second type of net—a *trammel*—when Jesus called them to be his disciples (Matt. 4:21).[18] The *seine* or *dragnet* is the third kind, and it may well be the oldest form of fishing net used in the Sea of Galilee.[19]

The seine is a special net that sports a long towline on each end. In order to deploy this net, the crew is divided into two groups. One remains on shore and secures one end of the net using one of the towlines while the remaining crew get into a boat and pull the net taut about fifty yards out into the lake. Floats on the top line of the net joined by weights on the bottom line keep the dragnet upright. Once the net is fully extended, the crew in the boat make a sweeping turn pulling the upright wall of the net in a semicircle back toward

Mending fishing nets in the early 1900s.

Courtesy of the House of Anchors Museum, Kibbutz Ein Gev.

Fisherman with St. Peter's Fish (Arabic *musht*, meaning "comb," referring to the shape of the dorsal fin).
© Direct Design.

shore. With the boat secured, the reunited crew uses both towlines to pull the arcing net toward the shoreline, corralling and entangling fish as it goes.[20]

Once the net is on shore, the work has just begun. The dragnet is an indiscriminate gatherer, and as a result it draws in a wide variety of fish, some of which cannot be eaten in accordance with Jewish dietary law. Fish that have dorsal fins and scales are approved to be eaten; those without dorsal fins or scales have to be discarded (Lev. 11:9–12). Consequently, once the fishermen have pulled in the net to the shore, it is necessary to separate the "good" fish from the "bad" fish.

Using this information, Jesus provided a parable about catching all kinds of fish and then separating the good fish from the bad (Matt. 13:47–48). The parable contains a number of details that call to mind fishing with a dragnet. In the parable Jesus linked the final activity of the fishing process with the end of the age. He pointed out an important similarity between what the fishermen in the parable had been doing and what would happen in the Kingdom of God. Just as fishermen spread nets, gathered fish, and sorted them, so the angels will gather and separate for God those who have been made righteous by him.

Catch of sardines from the Sea of Galilee.

A biny, or barbel, is a species of carp with what looks like barbs or whiskers at the corners of its mouth.

A LOST SHEEP IN OPEN COUNTRY

MATTHEW 18:1–14

esus's disciples were having a discussion about the question, "Who is the greatest in the kingdom of heaven?" (Matt. 18:1). From their perspective, children were not even in the running (Matt. 19:13).[21] So Jesus made a remarkable statement about the value of all people by taking a child, so lightly esteemed by these men, and saying, "Whoever humbles himself like this child is the greatest in the kingdom of heaven" (Matt. 18:4). Referring to the children in his presence, Jesus continued to teach about the Kingdom of God using the parable of the lost sheep—a parable set in the open country for a reason.[22]

Any of Jesus's illustrations that referred to sheep used a well-known cultural experience of his listeners. These animals were described in Scripture as ritually clean (Lev. 11:1–8) and were an important part of Jewish society.[23] Nearly every family had

contact with sheep and knew the daily rhythm of a sheep's life.

When darkness set in, the shepherd brought the sheep into an enclosure—either natural or manmade—in order to keep the vulnerable animals safe from thieves and predators (John 10:1–10). During the daylight hours the sheep were taken into the open country to feed. The open country was not a safe place for the flock because there the sheep were more vulnerable to the attack of wild animals. Thus they lived their lives between the safety of the overnight enclosure and the risk of the open country. Nevertheless, as long as it was daylight and the sheep remained together under the protecting hand of the shepherd (Ps. 23:4), the risk of being in the open country was kept at a minimum. This set the stage for the events in the parable Jesus told.

In this parable, the shepherd had led his flock into the hilly, open country where a very difficult situation developed (Matt. 18:12). One of his hundred animals wandered away. Since sheep have no means for defending themselves, when

Shepherdess leading her flock through the Judean Wilderness.

Wolf from southern Israel. Jesus often referred to those attempting to destroy his flock as wolves. © Direct Design.

Judean leopard. Sheep that get separated from the shepherd and flock are vulnerable to wild predators such as this one. © Direct Design.

one becomes separated from the shepherd and the flock its chances of survival are minimal. So what was the shepherd to do? The open country was where his sheep were most at risk. Was it worth putting the rest of the flock in harm's way in order to rescue one sheep? The shepherd chose to seek that lost sheep, and when he recovered it he had more joy over finding that one sheep than over the ninety-nine that had not wandered off (Matt. 18:13).

As Jesus applied this parable to the question of social rank, the sheep represented a child. Just as the shepherd was not willing to lose one sheep, Jesus said, "In the same way your Father in heaven is not willing that any of these little ones should be lost" (Matt. 18:14). If God shows this kind of concern for children, we can be assured that neither social nor cultural status determines or diminishes our value in his eyes.

Shepherdess carrying a lamb back to the flock.

© Direct Design.

EXTRAORDINARY RESCUE IN AN ORDINARY HOME

LUKE 15:1–10

*P*harisees and teachers of the law frequently disparaged Jesus for spending time with those who lived on the margins of religious acceptability—particularly the tax collectors and sinners. When those kinds of people gathered around Jesus, the Pharisees and teachers of the law muttered, "This man welcomes sinners and eats with them" (Luke 15:2). When Jesus heard this criticism from these religious leaders, he responded by telling them a series of parables designed to illustrate God's perspective of the value of the tax collectors and sinners. One of these was the parable of the lost coin.

It is important to note that in Luke's Gospel, this parable immediately followed one in which a shepherd rejoiced over finding his lost sheep. Jesus concluded that "in the same way there will be more rejoicing in heaven over one sinner who repents than over ninety-nine righteous persons who do not need to repent" (Luke 15:7). Similarly, Jesus used the parable of the lost coin to show the rejoicing over that which was lost being found, but in this parable he placed a slight difference in the conclusion. In the coin parable he spoke of a woman who lost one of ten silver coins. This coin referred to in the parable is called a *drachma*, worth approximately a day's wage. Since her coins represented about ten days' wages, it is thought that she lived in an ordinary village home consisting of limited light and compacted dirt floors.[24] Finding her small lost coin under those conditions was probably not a simple task. Therefore, when she found the lost coin, she was so thankful and excited that she called all of her friends and neighbors together to rejoice with her.

So in the minds of the Pharisees and teachers of the law, how did the

Greek silver drachma. A drachma such as this one was the missing object mentioned in the parable of the lost coin.

conclusion of the woman's recovery of her lost coin in her village home differ from the conclusion of the parable of the lost sheep? Sheep were animals that had the capacity to return to the flock on their own, which is what the Pharisees and teachers of the law expected of the tax collectors and "sinners." The religious leaders believed these outcasts had committed wrongs against other people for which restitution had to be made before forgiveness could be granted (see Luke 19:8).[25] Offenses between

Dining area of a Galilean home.

people had to be rectified between the parties involved, and forgiveness could not be granted, even by God on the Day of Atonement, until the transgression had been appeased.[26] The idea that people might forgive, much less seek out those who had wronged them, before the offense had been rectified was inconceivable to the Pharisees and teachers of the law. For them such restitution was the definition of repentance.

The lost coin, which in the parable represented the tax collectors and sinners, was incredibly valuable to its owner, even though it did not have the capacity to return (repent) to its owner as the sheep in the previous parable could. So when Jesus compared repentance of the tax collectors and sinners with the joy of an ordinary woman finding a lost coin, the religious leaders were stunned because Jesus's parable redefined repentance from their definition (an act of restoration made by the sinner) to God's definition (the act of being found even though the "coin" could do nothing to be found).

Basement of a Judean house. Searching for a lost coin in the basement, where animals were kept, would be no small task.

Kitchen and sleeping area of an ordinary Judean home.

A NEIGHBOR ON THE JERUSALEM-JERICHO ROAD

LUKE 10:25–37

Jesus's parables were most often delivered when he was speaking to a group of people such as the Pharisees or his disciples. One of the best known of these is the parable of the good Samaritan. Jesus used this story to explain God's perspective on love to an expert in Jewish law.

In this parable a Jewish man had a terrible experience while traveling on the road from Jerusalem to Jericho. He was attacked by robbers who stripped him, stole his belongings, and beat him nearly to death. Subsequently two Jewish men, first a priest and later a Levite, happened upon the wounded countryman. For reasons that are not given, both men stepped to the far side of the path and moved on. Then a third stranger came upon the scene. Because he was a Samaritan, he was the least likely of the three to offer assistance.[27] Despite the rancor that existed between Jews and Samaritans (John 4:9), this compassionate stranger offered the injured man support and assistance (Luke 10:33–35).

The parable of the good Samaritan is set on the Jerusalem-Jericho road that made its way for about fifteen miles through the difficult terrain of the Judean Wilderness. It descended nearly thirty-four hundred feet en route to the Jordan River valley.[28] Travel on most roads in the ancient world was hazardous, but that was particularly the case with this roadway. In the warmer months, intense heat and lack of water in the wilderness[29] threatened the traveler with dehydration. Besides natural perils, there was the risk of falling into the hands of robbers who used the landscape as a refuge.

With that in mind, the setting for this parable made two important contributions we do not want to miss. In the first case, we note that the priest who passed by was "going down" the road (Luke 10:31). While on the way to the Temple in Jerusalem, priests needed to be very careful not to ritually defile themselves. Contact with a man near death could potentially make a priest

Foundation of the Roman road connecting Jericho to Jerusalem.

ritually unclean, which in turn would interfere with his ability to carry out Temple assignments.

Likewise, Levites had similar concerns of ritual impurity because they assisted the priests. However, neither the Levite nor the priest in the parable was going to Jerusalem; they were going to Jericho (Luke 10:30–32). This disregard of the injured man is so unexpected because they were "going down" to Jericho. Therefore, any potential defilement would not affect their ability to

Terrain through the Judean Wilderness ▶
on the road between Jerusalem and Jericho.

function in the Temple. Yet they did not stop to help out this fellow son of Abraham.

As for the Samaritan, stopping to assist the injured Jewish man slowed his own trip through hostile terrain. Being delayed on this road put him at greater risk of being robbed by the same thieves who had descended on the man he was helping. So Jesus asked the expert in Jewish law, "Which of these three do you think was a neighbor to the man who fell into the hands of robbers?" The expert answered, "The one who had mercy on him" (Luke 10:36–37). In this parable Jesus provided a clear illustration of God's perspective on what it means to "love your neighbor" and told the expert in the law to "go and do likewise" (Luke 10:37).

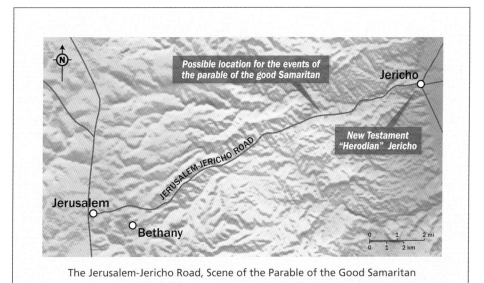

The Jerusalem-Jericho Road, Scene of the Parable of the Good Samaritan

JESUS IS THE GATE

JOHN 10:1–18

The inspired authors of the Bible frequently mention sheep and shepherds. Abraham, Moses, and David all took their turn at the head of the flock. When David left his family's sheep on the hillsides to lead Israel as their king, his new occupation was pictured in terms of his former life's work. God told him, "You will shepherd my people Israel" (2 Sam. 5:2). Of course God's people awaited their ultimate King, whom God also depicted as a shepherd through his prophet Ezekiel (Ezek. 34:11–16, 23–24). So from time to time Jesus spoke of himself and his role in pastoral terms. Perhaps the most striking example of that comes to us in John 10 where Jesus called himself the Good Shepherd who is the gate of the sheepfold.

This particular discussion was motivated by the circumstances of an unfortunate man who had been born blind, was healed by Jesus, and then was threatened with expulsion from the local synagogue by the religious leaders (John 9). These men conducted rigorous interviews designed to undermine the impact of this healing and discredit Jesus, the Light of the World (John 9:5), for helping the blind man on the Sabbath. While being interrogated, the parents of the man Jesus healed feared the Pharisees would expel them from the synagogue, which was a powerful threat because it would make them social outcasts in Jewish society.[30]

This is where Jesus referred to the cultural experience of tending sheep. His listeners knew that sheep were defenseless, which made them easy prey for the predators that roamed the open country where the flocks grazed.[31] Because nighttime posed the greatest risk, the shepherd brought his vulnerable flock into a protected and enclosed area referred to as a sheepfold. The sheepfold in the open country was either a natural cave or a circular enclosure built from fieldstones. Of course the space restrictions imposed on the flock by such an enclosure limited movement of the animals and therefore made it easier for thieves or predators to do their worst. That is why the shepherd remained with the sheep; after herding them into the sheepfold, he slept in the entry, functioning as its gate.

As Jesus spoke to the man who had his blind eyes opened, he used images from pastoral life. Note that he related the Pharisees who had expelled this man from the synagogue to hired shepherds who had gone bad.[32] He used even more critical language by likening them to thieves and robbers who made an illicit entry into the

Shepherd taking sheep to the sheepfold.

© Direct Design.

sheepfold (John 10:1). Their calloused attitudes and hostile behavior reflected an attempt to rob this believing and seeing "sheep" of his position within Jesus's fold. These men were not at all like the good shepherd who was committed to the security of his flock (John 10:11).

Referring to himself as the gate, Jesus guarded access to his beloved sheep, not allowing entry to anyone who meant them harm. He alone was the one who controlled the gate that led to life, protection, and eternal rescue. "I am the gate; whoever enters through me will be saved" (John 10:9). Thus the man who had been expelled from the synagogue was now offered reassurance by the Good Shepherd.

Sheep entering the sheepfold.

Sheep enter the opening of the sheepfold, where the shepherd then sits or lies down, thus becoming the "gate" of the sheepfold.

© Direct Design.

HEROD, JERICHO, AND THE KINGDOM

LUKE 19:11–27

esus spoke often and passionately about the Kingdom of God, asserting in no uncertain terms that it had come (e.g., Luke 8:1; 9:2, 27). This led some of his listeners to conclude that the full realization of the Kingdom of God was about to appear (Luke 19:11), so Jesus told the parable of the ten minas in order to explain the ultimate realization of his Kingdom.

Some maintain the parable of the ten minas is a thinly veiled reference to the lives of Herod the Great and his son Archelaus, who each functioned as one of the puppet kings of Israel, which at that time was under Roman domination.[33] Both Herod the Great and a generation later Archelaus left for Rome amid great opposition in order to obtain the crown. Similarly, both returned to put down rebellions that had escalated during their absence.[34]

In this parable of the ten minas, a man of noble birth left for a distant country to be appointed king. While he was away, opposition to his kingship arose (Luke 19:12, 14). This in no way prevented the coronation from occurring, and when this king returned, he dealt a fatal blow to those who opposed him (Luke 19:27). The succession to the throne of Herod the Great and Archelaus lend historical similarities to the parable, and the location in which Jesus spoke provided a geographical relationship as well.

Jesus told the parable immediately after speaking with Zacchaeus in Jericho,[35] a city that had an important connection to Herod the Great.

Jericho Hasmonean palace (view looking north).

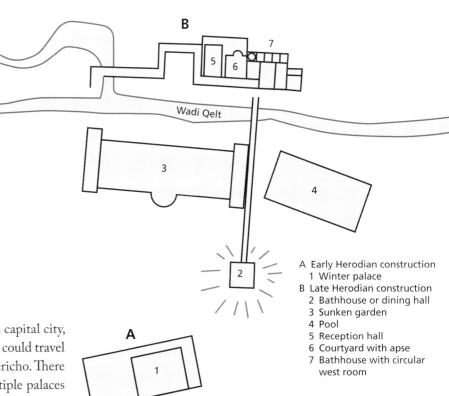

A Early Herodian construction
  1 Winter palace
B Late Herodian construction
  2 Bathhouse or dining hall
  3 Sunken garden
  4 Pool
  5 Reception hall
  6 Courtyard with apse
  7 Bathhouse with circular
     west room

Schematic of Herodian Palaces at Jericho

Although he had built up Jerusalem as his capital city, when the cold of winter settled in there, he could travel a day's journey to the warmer climate of Jericho. There he had built a complex that included multiple palaces with luxurious halls, a bathhouse, swimming pools, a sunken garden, a hippodrome, and a theater.[36] It was as though one had stepped from the barren realms of the Judean Wilderness into a type of Rome itself. After his father's death, Archelaus was granted the domain once held by Herod the Great, which included Jericho.

When Jesus passed through Jericho, the people listening to his teachings began to think that the Kingdom of God was going to appear immediately since he was near Jerusalem (Luke 19:11). So in this setting at Jericho, Jesus told the parable of the ten minas, which brought back to his listeners memories about Herod the Great and his son Archelaus.

The parable, however, was not a one-to-one correlation between Herod's situation and that of Jesus but rather an illustration of what was to come through a comparison and contrast between Herod and Jesus. Herod, and later his son Archelaus, had to go to Rome to get their authority to rule; Jesus came from God and already had legitimacy. Herod and Archelaus put Jerusalem's chief priests into power; Jesus revealed those chief priests to be false shepherds of Israel. The kingships of Herod and Archelaus were opposed by their subjects; Jesus was loved by the multitudes, who wanted to make him king (John 6:15). When Herod and Archelaus

returned after their coronation, they eliminated those subjects who opposed them; Jesus warned in this parable that upon his return, political and religious realms that opposed him would be destroyed. As he traveled from Herod's city of Jericho to the Temple in Jerusalem, that point would be etched into the minds of his listeners.

◀ Former swimming pool at Second Temple Jericho, the possible location of the drowning of Aristobulus III, son of Herod the Great and Mariamne.

The hippodrome at New Testament Jericho, where Herod the Great detained popular rabbis prior to his death.

THE FATHER'S HOUSEHOLD HAS MANY ROOMS

JOHN 14:1–3

or the disciples, reassurance was in order. Jesus had just told these men that he was getting ready to leave them, that they were about to disown him, and that he was going to surrender himself for execution. Even though the disciples' understanding of their rabbi had grown, as had their faith, this was hard news. It is no wonder that their hearts were troubled (John 14:1). Jesus called for them to trust him because he was going to his household (Greek, *oixia*, meaning "house," "home," or "family") in heaven where his Father had many places to live (Greek, *mone*, meaning "dwelling place") and in which he would prepare a place (Greek, *topos*, meaning "space" or "place") for them (John 14:1–2). The setting of their Passover meal—the guest room of someone else's house—amplified the meaningfulness of Jesus's declaration.

With the exception of Peter's relatives in Capernaum (Matt. 8:14), whenever we find Jesus and the disciples entering a house, it usually belonged to someone other than themselves.[37] Jesus came to earth where "foxes have holes and birds of the air have nests, but the Son of Man has no place to lay his head" (Matt. 8:20). As Jesus and his disciples walked from one community to the next proclaiming the arrival of God's Kingdom, they often stayed with listeners who opened their homes to them (Luke 10:5–7). Someone else's large upper room (Luke 22:12) provided the setting in which Jesus assured his disciples that he was going to his family home (*oixia*) and would prepare a place (*topos*) in his dwelling place (*mone*) for them.

Bible translators have struggled to find the appropriate words to translate John 14:2 because the family culture and house construction during the Gospel period was so different from our own. This verse speaks about his Father's house (Greek, *oixia*; Hebrew, *bet ab*), meaning "a multiple-family household consisting of blood relatives as well as the women connected through

Korazin *insula* home. The Greek word *mone* refers to a dwelling place similar to a home.

marriage."[38] The Mishnah records that a large house was twelve by fifteen feet.[39] Typical houses consisted of one primary room with a few ancillary rooms for storage.

During the time of the Gospels, people derived economic benefits and heightened personal security by living together in larger family units.[40] Consequently, compounds were formed that consisted of multiple houses or rooms. When a son married, he expanded his father's existing household by preparing a house or room for his new family.[41]

An eating room in the reconstructed Galilean village of Qatzrin. The Greek word *topos* could refer to an addition to the house or a specific room of the house.

Storage room in a Galilean village home.

Work on a room addition in the reconstructed Galilean village of Qatzrin.

The Rescuer was about to finish what he had come to do. "Jesus knew that the time had come for him to leave this world and go to the Father. Having loved his own who were in the world, he now showed them the full extent of his love" (John 13:1). He told them, "And if I go and prepare a place for you, I will come back and take you to be with me that you also may be where I am" (John 14:3). This declaration promised hope for the disciples that he would take them to live with their Redeemer (Job 19:25–27; Isa. 63:16) and be forever united with the Father (John 17:23–24).

The village of Ephraim (modern Taybeh). The Greek word *oixia* could refer to a village or tribe in which the people are all related.

GLORIFYING GOD
AND THE VINEYARD

JOHN 15:1–17

As Jesus continued to teach his final lessons, he spoke to his disciples using the image of a gardener, a grapevine, and its branches. "I am the true vine, and my Father is the gardener. . . . You are the branches" (John 15:1, 5). Jesus employed this image at that time for a reason.

The climate and topography of the Promised Land are exceedingly favorable for growing grapevines. As a result, in Bible times almost every village in the hill country was surrounded by vineyards and had at least one winepress for processing the grape harvest.[42] But even today, despite more favorable growing conditions, the grapevine remains one of the most demanding of all crops to grow, requiring significantly more time and attention than wheat or olives.[43]

The purpose of planting the vineyard was to produce grapes. In Jesus's illustration, God the Father is the Gardener who does everything possible in order to ensure good fruit. The tasks required of the gardener included preparing the field by removing the large stones, which were then used to build terraces. Moreover, the gardener

Vineyard terrace wall and hedge.

built watchtowers and winepresses (Isa. 5:2) and then planted the choicest vines. Knowing that the grapes might become sour as a result of dewfall if they were lying on the ground, the gardener placed a large rock under each cluster to lift the grapes off the soil. As the vines grew, he meticulously pruned the vines, removing unproductive branches, which in turn stimulated greater fruit production from the other branches of the vine.[44] The gardener then piled the pruned grapevines on top of the rock terrace wall in order to build an ancient form of barbed-wire fence in an attempt to protect the vineyard from unwanted animals entering the vineyard and decimating the produce. After the grape harvest the women gathered the pruned grapevines from the terrace walls and burned them as fuel for baking and for warmth in the winter.

Continuing his illustration, Jesus described himself as the vine and his disciples as the branches (John 15:5). Like the branches, if the disciples were disconnected from the loving care of the Gardener and from the nourishment of the vine, they would have no life or fruit. So Jesus said, "No branch can bear fruit by itself;

Judean vineyard. In Bible times, grapevines grew on the ground.

Agricultural watchtower built for the vineyard. ▶

it must remain in the vine. Neither can you bear fruit unless you remain in me" (John 15:4).

Jesus then said, "This is to my Father's glory, that you bear much fruit, showing yourselves to be my disciples" (John 15:8). The reason God (the Gardener) is glorified when the branch bears much fruit is because the branch had nothing to do with the growth of the fruit—it is all the doing of the Gardener. Thus Jesus used this common image to teach and encourage the disciples because he knew the difficulty they were about to encounter. The disciples could not withstand the dreadful hours that lay ahead on their own power, but there was assured hope—to abide in the vine. Therefore Jesus's words to the disciples were a reminder that any life they wished to have could be sustained only if they remained in him. It was the fruit of love that would prove them to be his disciples, and they could only have this love because of their heavenly Father's work as the Gardener (John 15:8–9).

Grapes near harvest time growing in a vineyard.

PART 4

JESUS IN THE WORLD OF THE GENTILES

Theater at Sepphoris, the capital of Galilee before AD 19.

Jesus was raised in an observant Jewish home in the small Jewish village of Nazareth. He spent time in the synagogue there and regularly traveled to the Temple in Jerusalem. When we trace his footsteps throughout the Gospels, we most often find ourselves in Jewish settings listening as Rabbi Jesus speaks to his fellow Israelites. That all seems fitting given the fact he is revealed to be the Messiah foretold in the Scriptures.

God intended for his Kingdom to include all peoples—Jews and Gentiles (Isa. 42:1–4; Matt. 12:17–21). The book of Acts in particular proclaims that the Kingdom of God was to spread in ever-widening circles from Jerusalem, to Judea, to Samaria, and finally to the ends of the earth (Acts 1:8). Jesus asserted the fact that Gentiles could be included in God's Kingdom even in the midst of his outreach to the lost sheep of the house of Israel. How did he teach that truth to the Jewish population, most of whom thought that Gentiles could not enter the Kingdom of God?

First, Jesus linked himself to the great prophets of Scripture who were messengers to Gentiles. That was certainly true of Jonah. We know more about his time in Nineveh than we do about his preaching among his fellow Israelites. When asked for a sign, Jesus directly connected himself to Jonah and thus to God's compassionate outreach to people outside of the sons of Abraham. He also linked himself with Elisha by healing a Samaritan man of leprosy on the road to Dothan near the location where Elisha encountered Naaman, the Aramean commander (2 Kings 5).

At other times Jesus went into the world of the Gentiles when he traveled to cities and regions whose dominant population was Gentile. Although these excursions into the Gentile world did not dominate his itinerary, they are present in Scripture and make his perspective clear. In part 4 we follow Jesus into the Gentile world, including such places as Samaria, the region of Tyre and Sidon, and the Decapolis.

Two important cities in Galilee—Sepphoris and Tiberias—had a strong Hellenistic and Gentile orientation. Yet the Gospels do not record that these two places were included in Jesus's itinerary. Thus part 4 will look at possible reasons why these two cities may not have received a visit from the Messiah.

These places we will review were immersed in a Gentile mind-set, although not all to the same degree. Whether Jesus was making himself known as the Messiah, rebuking his disciples for wanting to call fire down on a Samaritan village, commending a Canaanite woman for her great faith, leading his disciples on a trip to the *other side* of the Sea of Galilee, or watching his disciples collect seven baskets of leftover food, Jesus made it clear that Gentiles were welcome in the Kingdom of God and included in the promise of God's restoration of all humanity through himself, the promised Redeemer.

The Decapolis city of Gerasa (Jerash) in modern-day Jordan.

Relief of Assyrian aggression. Jonah was instructed to proclaim the Lord's mercy to the Assyrians.

Ephesian Artemis (first century).

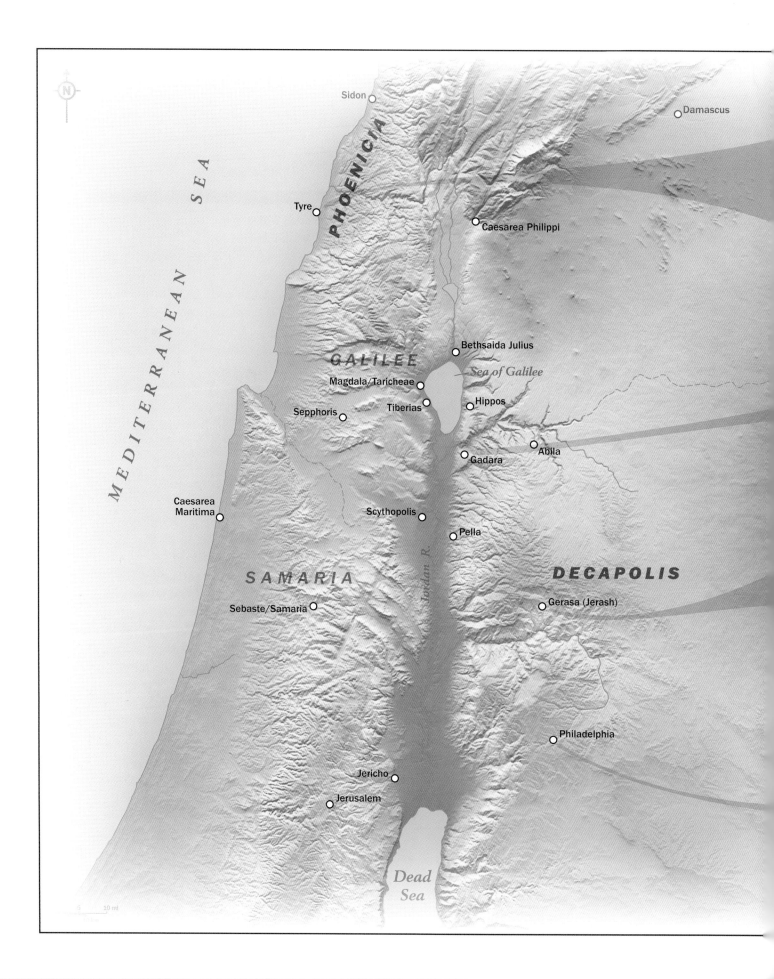

Excavations of the gymnasium at Tyre.

Excavations at the Decapolis city of Gadara, located in modern-day Jordan.

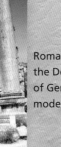

Roman temple in the Decapolis city of Gerasa (Jerash in modern-day Jordan).

Citadel at the Decapolis city of Philadelphia (modern-day Amman, Jordan).

JESUS, JONAH, AND THE NAZARETH RIDGE

MATTHEW 12:22–41

The connection between Jesus, Jonah, and the Nazareth Ridge surfaced in the middle of a heated exchange between Jesus and certain Pharisees and teachers of the law. Although these opponents had already begun to plot how they might kill Jesus (Matt. 12:14), they continued to shadow his every move and looked for ways to discredit his actions. In the context of this passage, Jesus had just healed a demon-possessed man. He maintained that this miracle was a sign that the Kingdom of God had come (Matt. 12:28), while the Pharisees and teachers of the law thought it proved Jesus was using power derived from the prince of demons (Matt. 12:24). As these men asked for a better sign, Jesus linked himself to Jonah and to the Nazareth Ridge for a reason.

View looking north from the Jezreel Valley to the Nazareth Ridge.

The request of these religious leaders will strike us as rather odd until we examine the finer nuances of their request. Jesus had just performed a striking miracle. So why did these men ask to see a "miraculous sign" (Matt. 12:38)? The answer lies in the Greek word at the heart of their request: *sēmeion*. In the ancient Greek translation of the first five books of the Bible (the Pentateuch of the Septuagint), this particular word appears again and again in reference to the miraculous signs God did through Moses to validate his credentials as God's messenger—the prophet God had sent to the Egyptians to demand the release of the Israelites.[1] Thus these opponents of Jesus were not merely asking for a miracle, they wanted a miraculous sign that proved Jesus was the fulfillment of the promise the Lord gave Moses in Deuteronomy 18:15, where Moses proclaimed, "The LORD your God will raise up for you a prophet like me from among your own brothers. You must listen to him." (See also John 1:45.)

Sarcophagus relief (fourth century) of the prophet Jonah.

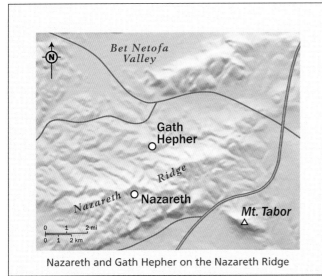

Nazareth and Gath Hepher on the Nazareth Ridge

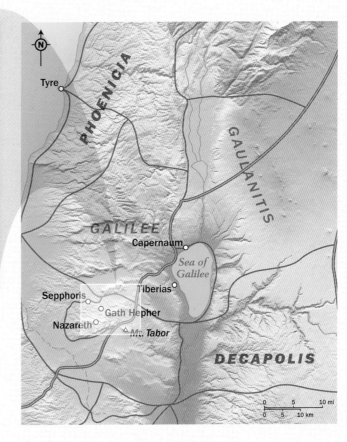

In reply to their request for a miraculous sign, Jesus turned their attention to Jonah and the Nazareth Ridge. Jesus and Jonah had something in common: both men had grown up within a few miles of one another, Jesus in Nazareth and Jonah in Gath Hepher (2 Kings 14:25).[2] As implied in the criticism of Nathanael, who came from nearby Cana (John 21:2), the Pharisees and teachers of the law probably assumed that it was highly unlikely for anything good to come out of the Nazareth area (John 1:46). Consequently the religious leaders wanted extra proof that Jesus was the prophet of God whom Moses proclaimed.

The validation Jesus offered addressed their concerns at several levels but in a way that they did not expect. He affirmed the fact that good things did come from the Nazareth region by pointing them to Jonah, "a Hebrew" who professed to "worship the Lord, the God of heaven, who made the sea and the land" (Jonah 1:9).[3] This man went into the Gentile city of Nineveh, called for them to repent, and witnessed a dramatic conversion of the Gentiles (Jonah 3). Jesus said, "For as Jonah was three days and three nights in the belly of a huge fish, so the Son of Man will be three days and three nights in the heart of the earth. The men of Nineveh will stand up at the judgment with this generation and condemn it; for they repented at the preaching of Jonah, and now one greater than Jonah is here" (Matt. 12:40–41). Since Jesus is greater than the prophet Jonah, this prophet from Nazareth would give even more compelling signs of his

origins (Deut. 18:15–18; Luke 24:44; John 7:40). After his crucified body was placed in a tomb, on the third day he would rise from the dead (Matt. 12:39–42).

Tell Gath Hepher (Khirbet ez-Zurrá, at top of hill behind white buildings), hometown of Jonah.

JESUS HAS TO TRAVEL THROUGH SAMARIA

JOHN 4:1–30

The Gospel writers frequently report Jesus's movement from one place to another with very mundane language. For example, "Jesus and his disciples went out into the Judean countryside" (John 3:22). In that light, the language of John's Gospel is surprising when he writes that Jesus "had to go through Samaria" (John 4:4).[4] This unusually strong language raises an important question: why was it necessary for Jesus to travel through Samaria?

Perhaps the answer lies in the pragmatics of first-century travel. Jesus journeyed from one place to the next in the same way that his contemporaries did. For them walking was a chief means of travel. Consequently the route of first choice was usually the most direct unless it proved too problematic. When Jesus left Judea en route to the Galilee, a quick glance at a map shows that the most direct route was through the region of Samaria. Not even the social tension between Jews and Samaritans was enough to prevent Jews from traveling

on this road.[5] Yet it is unlikely that these travel issues justified John's emphatic language.

A better case for the necessity of Jesus's travel through Samaria can be made when we consider the relationship of this location to the promises and covenants in Scripture. On one occasion as Jesus traveled through Samaria, he stopped at Jacob's well near Sychar where he met a Samaritan woman and engaged her in conversation. Jacob's well was located a short walk from the ancient city of Shechem. These sites, located between Mount Gerizim and Mount Ebal, are part of a rich history linked to the Messiah's coming.

After the Lord called upon Abram to leave his homeland and travel to the Promised Land of Canaan, he again spoke to Abram in Shechem. There God assured Abram that this land that connected Africa, Asia, and Europe would be a podium for his family and that it would host the Messiah's promised rescue. Upon hearing the promise, Abram built a memorial altar at Shechem to connect these promises with that place (Gen. 12:3,

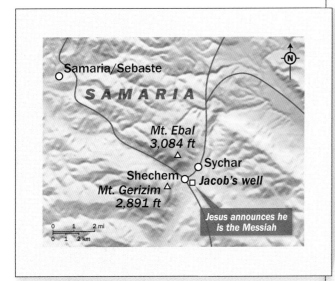

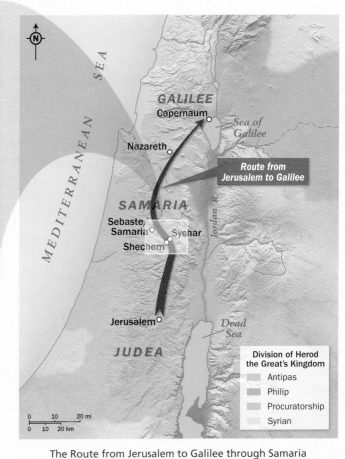

The Route from Jerusalem to Galilee through Samaria

6–7; John 8:56). Abram's family did become a great nation and experienced a lengthy stay in Egypt. But when the nation of Israel returned to the Promised Land under the leadership of Joshua, they returned not only with the promises extended to Abram but also with those they received at Mount Sinai. As Joshua led the Israelites back into the Promised Land, he honored the instructions Moses had given him. He took them to the valley between Mount Gerizim and Mount Ebal, built a memorial altar on Mount Ebal, and reviewed all the promises given to Moses and Abram (Deuteronomy 27–28; Josh. 8:30–35).

It was in this location brimming with anticipation of fulfilling God's promises to Abram and Moses that Jesus verbally proclaimed himself to be the Messiah: "The [Samaritan] woman said, 'I know that Messiah' (called Christ) 'is coming. When he comes, he will explain everything to us.' Then Jesus declared, 'I who speak to you am he'" (John 4:25–26). Thus it was no coincidence that Jesus readily revealed his identity as Messiah to the Samaritan woman, in the same location where God had previously established his promises to Abram and Joshua. Thus Jesus reminded the nation of Israel of those promises and others given to Moses.

◄ Samaria's Mt. Gerizim (left) and Mt. Ebal (right).

Jacob's well.

CROSSING ENEMY LINES TO THE *OTHER SIDE*

MARK 4:35–41

Jesus had been teaching at the Sea of Galilee and that evening instructed his disciples to get in the boats and travel with him to the *other side*. While en route to that destination, a sudden and horrible windstorm threatened to end the day in tragedy. We will see why a trip to the *other side* and this windstorm terrorized the disciples and how Jesus challenged them to turn that fear into faith in the one who came to usher in the Kingdom of God and overthrow the works of the adversary (1 John 3:8).

Jesus's invitation to board a boat and go to the *other side* must have stirred uncertainty in the disciples. Galilee's observant Jewish communities located on the northwest region of the Sea of Galilee were careful to eat only foods in accordance with Jewish dietary laws and avoid ritual impurity and idolatry of any kind.

These Jews wanted nothing to do with the Gentile population, especially those living on the southeast side (i.e., the *other side*) of the lake in the region of the Decapolis. The Greeks and later the Romans had built up the Decapolis cities to be showplaces of their authority and culture, including temples for the worship of idols, bath complexes, theaters, and stadiums. These things as

Capernaum with Mt. Hermon in the background (view looking north).

well as sexual promiscuity and a diet of pork and other ritually unclean foods were expressions of Satan's kingdom. From the perspective of observant Jews, no place could be further from the Kingdom of God.[6] Thus for them as for Peter, who up to this point had not entered the home of a Gentile (Acts 10:28), going to the *other side* was nothing less than crossing enemy lines into the realm of Satan.[7] Nevertheless, Jesus invited the disciples to trust his plan. The Kingdom of God would even include Gentiles who lived on the *other side*.

Boat from the first century BC.

While crossing the lake, an event seemed to validate the disciples' concerns. A windstorm developed that churned the waters of the lake so violently that the boat in which Jesus and the disciples rode began to fill with water. Usually these men were not afraid of traveling on the Sea of Galilee because a number of them were experienced fishermen. A late autumn and winter windstorm, called a *sharkia*,[8] can develop unexpectedly from the east side of the lake where higher elevations create a temperature inversion that leaves cold air on the ridges

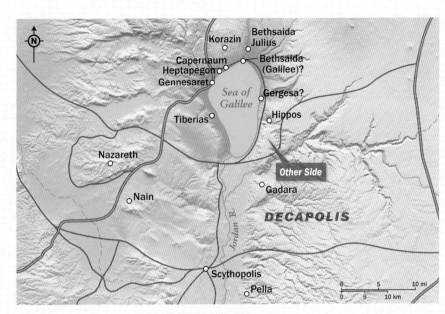

The *Other Side* of the Sea of Galilee

above and warm air in the lake basin 1,300 feet below. Within minutes, the waters of the lake can surge with six-foot and higher waves that can easily swamp the kind of boat transporting Jesus and the disciples (Mark 4:37).

Crossing into Satan's territory, Jesus turned the journey into an opportunity for the disciples to understand that God's Kingdom would in fact overthrow the kingdom of evil. The adversary was no match for the Son of God, even while Jesus slept at the rudder (Mark 4:38). With the authority of his word, Jesus commanded the chaotic waters to become calm. In awe, the disciples turned to one another and asked, "Who is this? Even the wind and the waves obey him!" (Mark 4:41).

Sea of Galilee (view looking north).

GREAT FAITH FOUND IN PHOENICIA

MATTHEW 15:21–28

Most of the time, Jesus proclaimed the Kingdom of God in the Promised Land among Jewish communities. People responded with faith, but Jesus did not often say that their faith was great. Consequently, it is striking when Jesus offers an incredible tribute to a Canaanite woman outside of Israel. She had come to Jesus requesting assistance for her demon-possessed daughter. After much persistence on her part, Jesus proclaimed, "Woman, you have great faith! Your request is granted" (Matt. 15:28).

Jesus and the disciples had traveled north to the Phoenician region that included the cities of Tyre and Sidon (Matt. 15:21). Evidence of a Jewish population living in Phoenicia extends back to when King David's son Solomon made an agreement with Hiram, king of Tyre, to supply lumber for building the Temple in Jerusalem. Solomon sent three shifts of ten thousand Israelite workers, with each group staying for one month at a time (1 Kings 5:14). Also, Huram of Tyre, whose mother was from the tribe of Naphtali and whose father was from Tyre (1 Kings 7:13–14), was named as assisting in bronze work for the Temple development. In the first century, the population of the region was still predominantly non-Jews who had adopted Greco-Roman culture and were not followers of the one true God.

The woman in this account was one of the non-Jews—a Gentile of Syro-

Coast of Tyre.

Phoenician ivory (eighth to ninth century BC).

Phoenician birth, a Canaanite (Matt. 15:21–22; Mark 7:26). That is why we find her language so dumbfounding. She addressed Jesus with what may well be the most Jewish of all titles: "Lord, Son of David" (Matt. 15:22). This title takes us back to the time when God promised King David that one of his descendants would be the Messiah (Acts 2:29–31).

Matthew's Gospel makes the point that the woman was not simply a Gentile; she was Canaanite. The fact that Matthew uses the term *Gentiles* numerous times[9] while using the term *Canaanite* only on this one occasion indicates its significance. So why does he focus on the woman's Canaanite heritage?

Earlier in their history, after their exodus from Egypt, the Israelites had come to the Promised Land—a place already inhabited by seven nations, including the Canaanites. Moses told his people that the Lord would drive those seven nations out of the land, and at that time the Israelites were to show those nations no mercy (Deut. 7:1–5). Keeping in mind Israel's history with Canaanites, it is not surprising that the disciples wanted

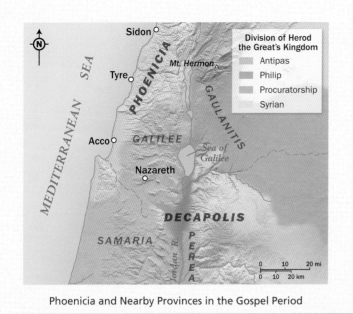
Phoenicia and Nearby Provinces in the Gospel Period

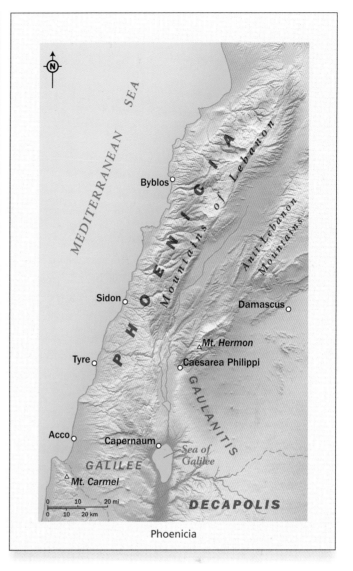
Phoenicia

nothing to do with this Canaanite woman who was considered a "dog" from the observant Jewish perspective (Matt. 15:23, 26).

According to Matthew's Gospel, up to this point Jesus had proclaimed the Kingdom of God to Galilee's observant Jews, Hellenized Jews, and even a God-fearing Gentile Roman centurion in the region of the Galilee. The news of the Kingdom of God was breaking out of all preconceived barriers. Who would be included next?

In Phoenician territory, this Canaanite woman approached Jesus. At first he seemed to respond by avoiding, ignoring, and then rejecting this Gentile woman's request: "It is not right to take the children's bread and toss it to their dogs" (Matt. 15:26). This remark can be understood in the context of Jewish prayers made over food. For some, once food had been blessed and dedicated to God, it should never be given to anyone or anything unclean, such as dogs, which would profane the dedicated food. But this Canaanite "dog" believed that Jesus, the Messiah, the Son of David, had the power to heal her daughter and that she, an unclean Canaanite woman, could be a recipient of the Lord's provisions: "Yes, Lord . . . but even the dogs eat the crumbs that fall from their masters' table" (Matt. 15:27). Her great faith resulted in a commendation from Jesus, and her daughter was healed.

Ptolemaic Phoenician inscription (221 BC).

SEVEN BASKETS
IN THE DECAPOLIS

MARK 8:1–21

*T*he details that comprise the feeding of the four thousand and the five thousand are strikingly similar (Mark 6:30–44; 8:1–21): a large crowd had gathered around Jesus, he took bread and fish and fed thousands, and afterwards the disciples gathered many baskets filled with leftovers. Therefore, when Jesus redirected the attention of the disciples to these two experiences, he urged them to take note of one important difference: the number of baskets they had collected (Mark 8:17–21). We will do the same as we turn our thoughts to the seven baskets the disciples gathered in the feeding of the four thousand.

That feeding took place on the southeast side of the Sea of Galilee in the region of the Decapolis (Mark 7:31) during a time when Jesus had withdrawn from the observant Jewish population that lived on the northwest side of the lake. The previous time Jesus crossed the Sea of Galilee and visited the Decapolis, the people there pleaded with him to leave (Mark 5:17). But in this visit they thronged around him[10] and were affirmed in their faith as Jesus provided them with a miraculous meal. It was after that meal that the disciples gathered the seven baskets.

Like other numbers used by the inspired writers of the Bible, the number seven can carry connotations that

The Decapolis city of Hippos (view looking north).

exceed its simple numeric value. While *seven* is often related to the concept of "completeness" or "totality,"[11] it is also a number associated with Gentiles. The latter is the association Jesus had in mind.

As he urged the disciples to reflect on these two miraculous feedings, Jesus called attention to the difference in the number of baskets that were collected (Mark 8:17–21). In the feeding of the five thousand, he had provided food for Jews who were headed to Jerusalem for the celebration of Passover.[12] The twelve baskets collected after feeding the five thousand affirmed that he had come to the lost sheep of the house of Israel—the number *twelve* had long been identified with the twelve tribes of Israel. As an example, note the twelve tribes of Israel (Gen. 49:28), twelve loaves (Lev. 24:5), and twelve thrones (Matt. 19:28). This unmistakable connection between those fed and the number of baskets collected points to the significance in the seven baskets collected during the feeding of the four thousand. The number *seven* was used in reference to the Gentile nations who lived in the Promised Land prior to the Israelites' arrival (Deut. 7:1; Acts 13:19).[13]

The excavations at the Decapolis city of Gadara (view looking northwest).

A view looking northeast toward the ruins of Scythopolis, illustrating ▶ the size and influence a Decapolis city had over its territory.

When we put it all together, we find a powerful message that links location and number. Jesus had miraculously fed two different groups of people in two different places. The difference in the number of baskets collected, together with the location of the miracles, emphasizes the identity of the two groups—one Jewish and the other Gentile. In these miracles Jesus fed both groups, providing them with spiritual and physical nourishment and thereby affirming that his eternal Kingdom includes Jews and Gentiles.[14]

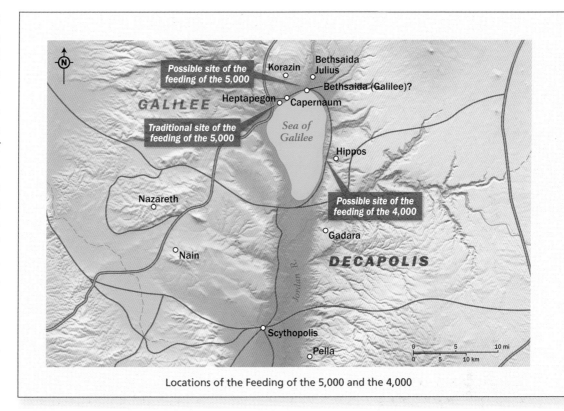

Locations of the Feeding of the 5,000 and the 4,000

JESUS VISITS THE REGION OF CAESAREA PHILIPPI

MATTHEW 16:13–23

The region around Caesarea Philippi witnessed an incredible event. When Jesus asked his disciples who they thought him to be, it was Simon Peter who voiced this powerful confession: "You are the Christ, the Son of the living God" (Matt. 16:16). The location combined with the words of Deuteronomy 32 show that Jesus visited the region of Caesarea Philippi for a reason.[15]

The language and themes of Deuteronomy 32 provide a backdrop for Jesus's visit. As Moses's life drew to a close (Deut. 31:14), the words of Deuteronomy 32 were likely his final address to the Israelites. Moses used a distinctive title for God, calling him "the Rock" (Deut. 32:4, 15, 18, 30–31) and describing how their Rock would bring his people to the region of Bashan and bless them with the bounty of that land (Deut. 32:14). To this day Bashan enjoys ample rainfall that combines with rich volcanic soil to produce incredible pastures and grain fields (Ps. 22:12; Ezek. 39:18).[16] But after God blessed Israel by putting such resources to work on their behalf, Moses prophesied that

Statuette of the idol Pan.

The cave (entrance into Hades), rocky facade, and temple to the idol Pan at Caesarea Philippi (view looking north).

the Israelites would forget the connection between those resources and the Rock who had provided them. In time, they would reject the Rock their Savior and replace him with foreign idols (Deut. 32:15–18).

As he neared Caesarea Philippi, Jesus was in the region of ancient Bashan described in Deuteronomy 32. The grain fields and pastures were still present, but so was the evidence that the people had forgotten God their Rock. Caesarea Philippi teemed with Roman idolatry: Herod the Great had built an imposing marble temple in honor of Caesar Augustus,[17] and a Roman temple dedicated to the idol Pan lay at the base of the rocky escarpment overlooking the city.[18] In addition, the Romans believed the large cave where sacrifices to demons were made, which was adjacent to the temple to Pan, was the gateway into Hades.[19]

So it was here in the ancient region of Bashan, within site of Mount Hermon, the highest mountain in the region, where Jesus focused on the word *rock* with his disciples. More specifically, it was at Caesarea Philippi, with its rocky facade overlooking the city, that Jesus proclaimed that from then on Simon would be called Peter (i.e., the *rock*) as a reminder that Satan's kingdom would be overthrown and the "gates of Hades" would not prevail against the fellowship of Jesus's followers (Matt. 16:18).

For the disciples, Jesus's proclamation of "the rock" in the region of Caesarea Philippi had a significant connection to Scripture. It lay in the words of the prophecy of Moses (Deuteronomy 32) to which Jesus could point concerning his upcoming rejection. The disciples were aware that God had brought ancient Israel into the land, including Bashan, where they then "abandoned the God who made [them] and rejected the Rock [their] Savior" by sacrificing to demons and worshiping idols (Deut. 32:15; see also vv. 15–18). So as he was in the region of Bashan in the vicinity of Caesarea Philippi's rock and the cave believed to be the "entrance into Hades," Jesus announced the coming of his ultimate rejection—the crucifixion (Matt. 16:18, 21).

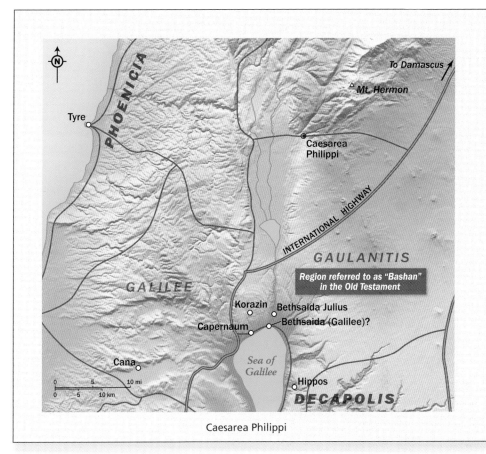

Caesarea Philippi

Caesarea Philippi temple niches for the idol Pan.

◀ Coin of Herod Philip (4 BC–AD 34), minted at Caesarea Philippi (Panias).

FIRE FROM HEAVEN ON A SAMARITAN VILLAGE

LUKE 9:51–55

Jesus and his disciples needed to travel between Galilee and Judea, which necessitated a trip through the region of Samaria. While they were traveling through that region, two of Jesus's disciples asked a most unexpected and puzzling question: "Lord, do you want us to call fire down from heaven to destroy them?" (Luke 9:54). James and John were speaking in reference to an unnamed Samaritan village whose inhabitants had refused to welcome him. This peculiar request from the disciples will be more understandable when we see that it happened in the region of Samaria for a reason.

The mention of fire from heaven takes us back to an event in Elijah's lifetime.[20] King Ahaziah had been seriously injured in a fall. Although he was the king of Israel, he sent messengers from his palace in Samaria to consult the idol Baal-Zebub at Ekron to inquire about his prognosis. Elijah intercepted the messengers and informed them that King Ahaziah would die (2 Kings 1:6; see vv. 2–6). In response, the king sent a captain and fifty

soldiers to arrest Elijah. Ahaziah had to send soldiers three times before Elijah was arrested because fire fell from heaven and consumed the first two groups (2 Kings 1:9–15).

James and John's inquiry about using destructive fire occurred near the place where Elijah had previously called down fire on the soldiers. It appears that Elijah intercepted the messengers of King Ahaziah shortly after they had left Samaria, sending them back to their king with a message from the Lord. When King Ahaziah's captains with their companies approached Elijah, he was sitting at the top of a hill.[21] This suggests that the fire from heaven fell in the geographical region of Samaria, which explains why James and John also raised the question about calling down fire to judge those in the Samaritan village who had not welcomed Jesus.

Jesus's rebuke (Luke 9:55) takes on meaning when we consider that he and his disciples had spent the

The hill of Samaria, also known as Sebaste (view facing north).

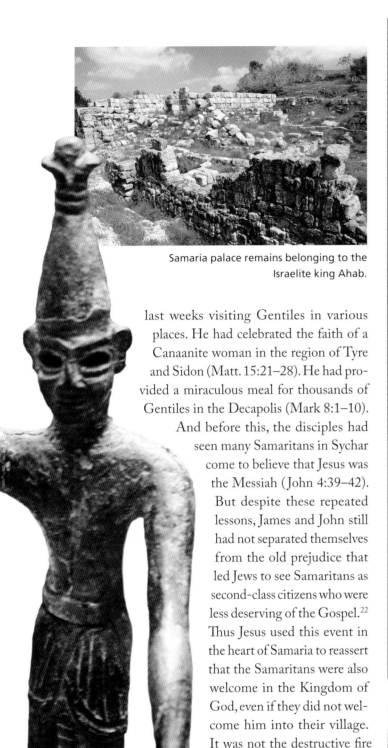

Samaria palace remains belonging to the Israelite king Ahab.

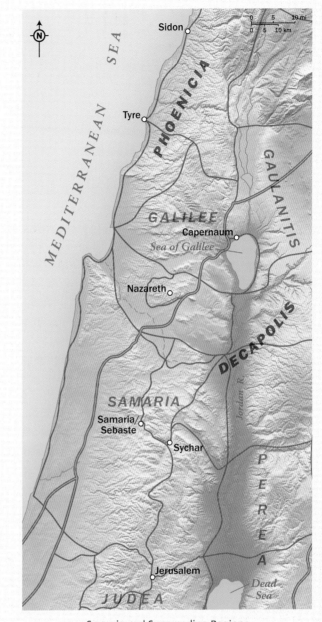

Samaria and Surrounding Regions

last weeks visiting Gentiles in various places. He had celebrated the faith of a Canaanite woman in the region of Tyre and Sidon (Matt. 15:21–28). He had provided a miraculous meal for thousands of Gentiles in the Decapolis (Mark 8:1–10). And before this, the disciples had seen many Samaritans in Sychar come to believe that Jesus was the Messiah (John 4:39–42). But despite these repeated lessons, James and John still had not separated themselves from the old prejudice that led Jews to see Samaritans as second-class citizens who were less deserving of the Gospel.[22] Thus Jesus used this event in the heart of Samaria to reassert that the Samaritans were also welcome in the Kingdom of God, even if they did not welcome him into their village. It was not the destructive fire from heaven but the revitalizing fire of God's Word that John (along with Peter) would carry to these Samaritans in the days following Jesus's ascension (Acts 8:14–17, 25).

Bronze Canaanite Baal idol.

Stairs that once led up to Herod the Great's temple at Sebaste that was dedicated to Caesar Augustus (Sebaste).

TEN LEPERS ON THE ROAD TO DOTHAN

LUKE 17:11–19

The Kingdom of God is even for the Samaritans. Luke works aggressively to make this point in his Gospel and in the book of Acts. In Acts, he describes how hundreds of Samaritans came to know Jesus as their Lord (Acts 8:4–25). His Gospel describes events that prepared Jesus's followers for the inclusion of Samaritans in the Kingdom of God.[23] That is clearly the case when a Samaritan—one of ten men healed of leprosy—was the only one who returned to thank Jesus (Luke 17:16). We will see how the location of this miracle illustrates God's compassion for Samaritans.

By the time of this event, the knowledge of Jesus's healing abilities had spread like wildfire among those with physical ailments. So when ten men afflicted with leprosy heard that he was coming their way, they shouted, "Jesus, Master, have pity on us!" (Luke 17:13). As this plea reached Jesus's ears, it touched his heart. But rather than healing the men on the spot, he told them to go and present themselves to the priests—men who doubled as public health inspectors within Jewish culture (see Lev. 13:2–46; 14:2–32). On the way all ten men were healed, but just one, who was described as a "Samaritan" and therefore a "foreigner," returned to offer Jesus his thanks (Luke 17:16–18).

Because the meeting between the Samaritan and Jesus occurred along the road to Dothan (Luke 17:11),[24]

Shepherd with his flock on the road near Dothan.

intersecting Samaria with Galilee, it brings to mind another Gentile who sought out a prophet to cure his leprosy in the same vicinity.[25] In 2 Kings we read about a commander of Aram's army who was afflicted with leprosy. On one of his raids against Israel, Naaman had captured a young Israelite girl whom he brought to his home to work for his wife. This young girl spoke to his wife about the power her God displayed through the prophet Elisha. If there was a prophet who could help Naaman, it was Elisha. With hope dawning on his despair, the leprous Naaman went to the home of Elisha and requested healing. But rather than healing him on the spot, Elisha sent the Aramean commander away to wash in the Jordan River. When Naaman did, he was healed. With a thankful heart, he returned to Elisha and declared, "Now I know that there is no God in all the world except in Israel" (2 Kings 5:15; see 2 Kings 5:1–16).

A link is forged by several similarities between Jesus's healing of this unnamed Samaritan and Elisha's encounter with Naaman the Syrian. Both recipients of healing were foreigners; both were lepers; both were sent someplace else for healing and obeyed; and both encounters occurred in the same region. Luke's record of

Tell Dothan (view looking southeast).

Temple model—the Chamber of Lepers to the right of Nicanor Gate. Jesus instructed the healed lepers to show themselves to the priests.

the Samaritan's healing and consequent gratitude near the place where Naaman had encountered Elisha and then affirmed his faith in the God of Israel confirms that acceptance of foreigners into the Kingdom was rooted in Scripture.

Welcoming Gentiles into the Kingdom of God was not a new precedent that began with Jesus's instructions and interactions with these lepers. He who said, "I and the Father are one," had always wanted to restore whoever would come (John 10:25–30), including Naaman the Syrian and the ten lepers (Luke 4:27).

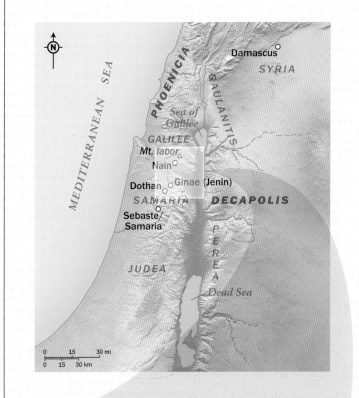

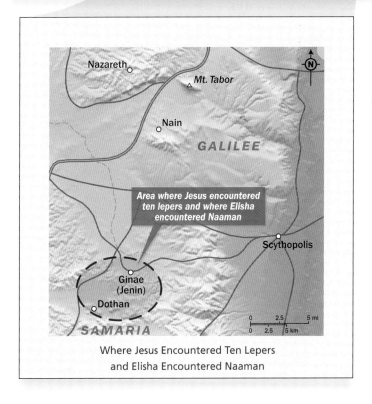

Where Jesus Encountered Ten Lepers and Elisha Encountered Naaman

Relief of a Syrian, or Aramean, king (eleventh century BC).

DID JESUS VISIT SEPPHORIS OR TIBERIAS?

JOHN 6:23

The Gospels name numerous places Jesus visited. As he moved back and forth throughout the Promised Land, two cities conspicuous by their absence from his recorded itinerary are the capital cities of Galilee: Sepphoris and Tiberias. Jesus did many miraculous signs in the presence of his disciples that are not recorded in Scripture (John 20:30; 21:24–25), yet it seems curious that no mention is made of Jesus going to either of Galilee's capital cities. A closer look at their history and culture provides clues to the pros and cons of Jesus going to either location.

The ruins of Sepphoris are located in Lower Galilee on a hill just a few miles north of Nazareth. Sepphoris was in a highly desirable location because of its access to abundant springs and to the fertile valleys around it. The city was also on more easily defendable high ground; consequently it was a valued military location and had a history of being fortified, conquered, and refortified many times prior to the first century AD.[26] By the close of the first century BC, Herod Antipas, son of Herod the Great, turned Sepphoris into a royal showplace, the largest city in the Galilee, and the political capital of the region.[27]

Antipas later moved the capital from Sepphoris when he laid the foundation for his new capital, a stunning embodiment of opulence that he named after the emperor Tiberius, who was his Roman benefactor (ca. AD 19). This city was on the west shore of the Sea of

Mosaic floor from a house in Sepphoris depicting a female in the famous *Acanthus Medallion*, which contains scenes from the life of Dionysus.

Galilee—a location that provided access to fresh water, hot springs, and a thriving fishing industry.

There are several reasons for Jesus to visit Sepphoris and Tiberias: He often taught in close proximity to these cities. He had grown up only a few miles from Sepphoris and passed near the city in order to get to Cana of Galilee. And he was in constant view and close proximity to Tiberias as he taught in other places around the Sea of Galilee.

Some interesting factors, however, might help explain Jesus's possible absence from both Sepphoris and Tiberias: Herod Antipas had built these cities both physically and ideologically to represent the best that the Greco-Roman world had to offer,[28] but cities with stadiums, theaters, and art dedicated to the idols of Rome were no place for observant Jews. All Jews were to be loyal to the God of Abraham, Isaac, and Jacob, representing and

View of Sepphoris looking northeast toward the Bet Netofa valley.

identifying with him in all manner of life, but these cities were populated by Hellenized Jews who had assimilated into the Greco-Roman culture that was pervasive throughout the Galilee. Moreover, it was Hellenized Jews who had achieved control of the Temple in Jerusalem by selling their birthright in exchange for political power from Rome.

Jesus went to the observant Jewish population centers to reveal himself as the Messiah. He crossed enemy lines to proclaim the Kingdom of God to Gentiles in the Decapolis. He even traveled to Phoenicia and brought mercy to Canaanites. But the Gospel writers do not record whether Jesus went to Sepphoris or Tiberias, two capital cities of the Galilee.

Excavations of Tiberias (view looking south).

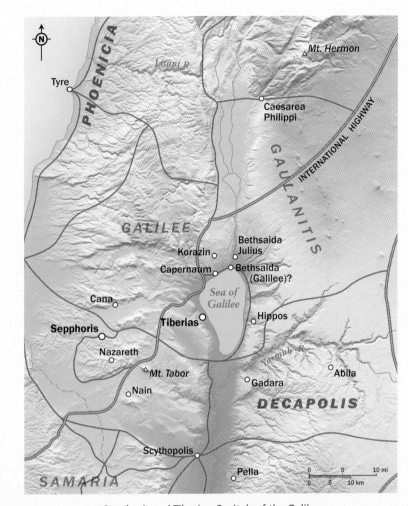

Sepphoris and Tiberias: Capitals of the Galilee

PART 5

JESUS IN AND AROUND JERUSALEM

View looking east over the Temple Mount and the western wall.

The Gospels indicate that Jesus traveled to the environs of Jerusalem at selected times for specific purposes. Part 5 will focus on the links between those times and purposes in relation to the locations and activities associated with his Jerusalem visits.

As we survey the times Jesus was in and around Jerusalem, we see that he came to this area for two important reasons. The first had to do with his mission to reclaim the Temple in Jerusalem from those who had perverted it for their own selfish gain. That is what lay behind Jesus's driving out the Temple merchants in the Royal Stoa (John 2:13–16). While this market could have functioned in a virtuous way, it did not. The severity of the corruption of the Temple aristocracy called for the cleansing words and actions of the Messiah. The same purpose also lay behind Jesus's trip to Jerusalem for the Feast of Dedication. At this festival that was meant to commemorate the Temple's purification, Jesus confronted the corrupt Temple leaders, exposing their fraudulent claims to the priesthood.

The second reason Jesus visited the environs of Jerusalem was to proclaim his messianic identity. When he went to the Feast of Tabernacles, he stood near the Water Gate of the Temple. At the very moment when others were reflecting on the anticipated arrival of the Messiah, Jesus's voice rang through the Temple courts: "Whoever believes in me, as the Scripture has said, streams of living water will flow from within him" (John 7:38).

Audiences in Jerusalem were divided in their opinions of Jesus's identity. That was partly because both the common people and the religious leaders in Judea questioned his Galilean background. We will explore why that proved to be an obstacle to Jesus's credibility.

As Jesus takes the final steps toward Jerusalem on the Jerusalem-Jericho road, we join him as he meets Bartimaeus. Jesus and Bartimaeus were drawn to this roadway for different reasons, but each left with something special. Bartimaeus had his sight restored; Jesus left with his true identity confirmed as Bartimaeus repeatedly called him the "Son of David." As we join Jesus in Jericho, we will also look at the encounter between him and the tax collector Zacchaeus.

In expressing himself as the Messiah, Jesus spent time in and around Jerusalem to clarify his authenticity to the Temple leadership. As he healed a disabled man at the Bethesda Pools and healed a blind man at the Pool of Siloam, he proclaimed a powerful message about his authority to the religious leaders in Jerusalem. Thus while Jesus spent more time in the northern portions of the Promised Land, his activities in and around Jerusalem served very important purposes that were all connected to that place.

Hannukia used in the celebration of the Feast of Dedication.

Mosaic of a *lulab* and citron used in the Feast of Tabernacles.

Jerusalem, with the Temple Mount at the center.

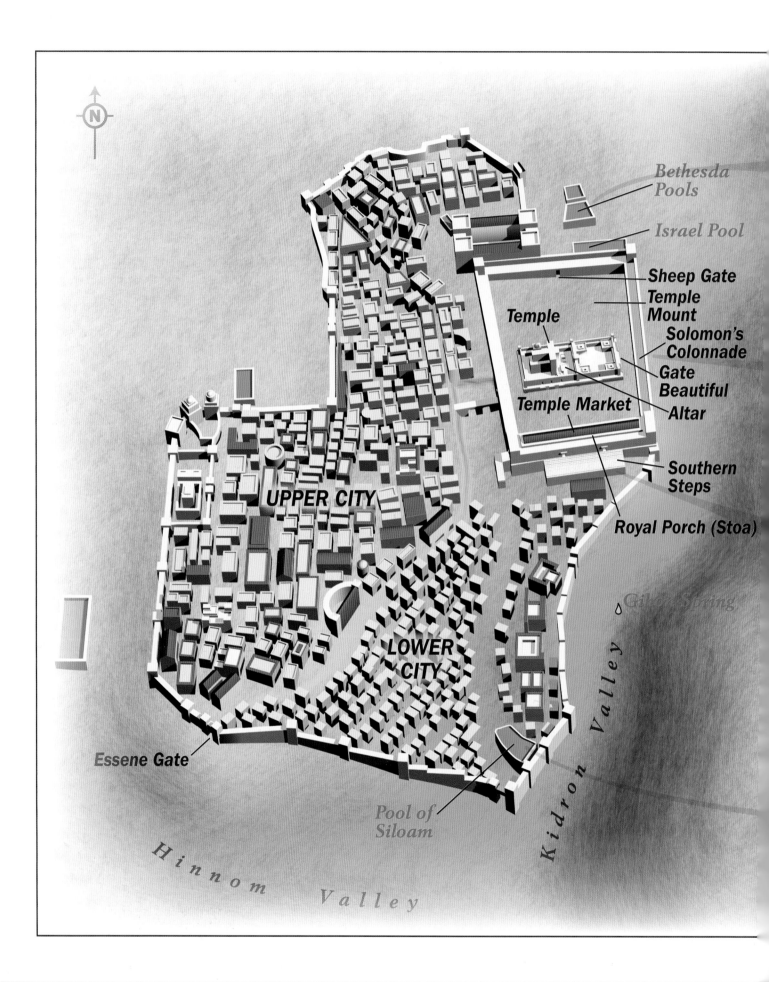

Bethesda Pools

Israel Pool

Sheep Gate

Temple Mount

Temple

Solomon's Colonnade

Gate Beautiful

Temple Market

Altar

Southern Steps

Royal Porch (Stoa)

UPPER CITY

LOWER CITY

Gihon Spring

Kidron Valley

Essene Gate

Pool of Siloam

Hinnom Valley

Excavations of the
Bethesda Pools.

Model depicting
Solomon's Colonnade.

© Dr. James C. Martin. Reproduction
of the City of Jerusalem at the time
of the Second Temple. (See full credit
on page 4.)

Model of the Pool
of Siloam.

Southern steps of the
Temple Mount (view
looking east).

© Dr. James C. Martin. Reproduction of the City of Jerusalem at the time
of the Second Temple. (See full credit on page 4.)

JESUS EXPELS THE TEMPLE MERCHANTS

JOHN 2:13–17

A memorable event from the life of our Savior took shape when he removed merchants from the Temple courts. Jesus took a whip, drove out the sheep and cattle, and overturned the tables of the money changers. He reprimanded those who sold doves, saying, "Get these out of here! How dare you turn my Father's house into a market!" (John 2:16). Jesus's bold condemnation took place in the public entry of the Temple complex for a reason.

The priestly aristocracy controlled and profited from the operation of the Temple. These men were not legitimate priests but were Roman appointees whose primary goal was to maintain their power base and increase their personal wealth.[1] The institution of the Temple provided them with a combination of financial, judicial, and religious power. In other words, the Temple functioned like today's Wall Street, Supreme Court, and Vatican all rolled up into one.

There were two ways in which the priestly aristocracy profited from the Temple. First, all sacrificial animals had to be approved by the aristocratic priesthood that controlled the Temple, and since they primarily approved

Jerusalem model—the Royal Stoa where Temple merchants did business (view looking southwest).

© Dr. James C. Martin. Reproduction of the City of Jerusalem at the time of the Second Temple. (See full credit on page 4.)

animals that they owned, sacrificial animals had to be purchased from them. Second, these same priests required that those animals could only be purchased with the high-silver-content Tyrian shekels, even though idolatrous images were on the coins. These shekels could be obtained only from the money changers who were also part of the aristocratic priestly families.[2]

Initially God had directed those coming to the tabernacle during the high festival of Passover to bring animals for sacrifice (Deut. 16:1–4). So in the period of the Gospels, the Temple aristocracy was misusing the

Relief of a money changer with his client (third century).

© Dr. James C. Martin. The British Museum. Photographed by permission.

worshipers by manipulating their Temple gifts and offerings.

These abuses associated with the Temple market took place before the eyes of all because they occurred within the halls of the Royal Stoa. Herod the Great had surrounded the Temple and its courts with a stoa (porch) that consisted of multiple rows of marble columns that supported a roof.[3] The Royal Stoa on the south side of the Temple complex was the largest and most ornate of them all, consisting of four rows of columns and comprising an area 607 feet by 74 feet.[4] Under the cover of this large and ornate structure—the main entrance to the Temple complex—is where the Temple market was located.[5]

Jesus chose this place to make a powerful public statement about what the priestly aristocracy was doing with his Father's house (John 2:16–17). Of course Jesus could have found a more private way to express his concerns. But instead he went into the Temple market located in the Court of the Gentiles, adjacent to the Royal Stoa—arguably the most populated spot in the Temple during Passover—and announced, "How dare you turn my Father's house into a market!" (John 2:16). His disciples remembered the prophecy, "Zeal for your house will consume me" (John 2:17). Moreover, this was a direct allusion to Jeremiah 7:11, "Has this house, which bears my Name, become a den of robbers to you? But I have been watching! declares the Lord." The Temple had been publicly shamed by those who should have guarded its purity. It belonged to Jesus's Father and so it belonged to him. The time to reclaim it had come.

Model of the Jerusalem Temple, with a view looking south toward the Royal Stoa (top of photo).

© Dr. James C. Martin. Reproduction of the City of Jerusalem at the time of the Second Temple. (See full credit on page 4.)

In the first century, sheep and goats were sold in the courtyard near the Royal Stoa.

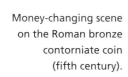

Silver drachma coin (350–325 BC) with banker's table (*trapeza*).

© Dr. James C. Martin. The British Museum. Photographed by permission.

Money-changing scene on the Roman bronze contorniate coin (fifth century).

© Dr. James C. Martin. The British Museum. Photographed by permission.

HEALING AT THE POOLS OF BETHESDA

JOHN 5:1–15

The definition of *Judaism* in the Gospel period was very diverse. There were Jewish people living in various cultures, speaking different languages, and holding different views of Scripture. So in this context, what held Judaism together in the first century? It was the Temple. The Temple defined Judaism, united Judaism, and provided means for the people to know God (Psalm 100; Luke 2:27–32, 37).

An overview of John's Gospel reveals that each time Jesus came to Jerusalem, he had a major conflict with a group called "the Jews" (see, for example, John 5:10). Since Jesus, his disciples, and the majority of participants in the Gospels were Jewish, a closer look at the phrase *the Jews* is warranted. What we find is that it is usually associated with events that occurred in the Temple environs, thereby connecting the use of *the Jews*

Model of the Bethesda Pools.

© Dr. James C. Martin. Reproduction of the City of Jerusalem at the time of the Second Temple. (See full credit on page 4.)

to the chief priests, teachers of the law, and elders of the people.[6] These men, who controlled the Temple and made up the Temple vanguard, came from one of two groups—the Sadducees (chief priests) or the Pharisees (teachers of the law and elders of the people).

It was by the Bethesda Pools in Jerusalem, located just a short distance to the north of the Temple complex, that the blind, lame, and paralyzed lay (John 5:3). So we will come to learn why Jerusalem's Temple leadership were so upset when Jesus healed the invalid at the Bethesda Pools, so close but so far away from the Temple.

John describes in some detail the location of the invalid's healing. It happened in Jerusalem near the Sheep Gate beside pools called Bethesda (John 5:2)[7] approximately one hundred yards north of the first-century Temple Mount. Here we find two rectangular pools separated by a wall twenty feet wide and surrounded by a colonnaded porch.[8]

The disabled man whom Jesus healed had come to these pools for a reason. This was the one place he dared to hope for help for the disability with which he had lived for thirty-eight years. Jesus came to the Bethesda Pools to address such hopelessness and to show the

Aerial view of the excavation of the Bethesda Pools and the Church of St. Anne's.

Excavated area of the Bethesda Pools.

Excavation of the Bethesda Pools in the foreground, with the Church of St. Anne's in the background.

people of Jerusalem yet another illustration of the Kingdom of God.

Although the disabled of Jerusalem were near the Temple, the focus of their hope was not in that direction. We get an example of the religious leaders' attitude toward those gathered by the pool after Jesus healed the disabled man. These religious leaders were more interested in criticizing the man for carrying a mat on the Sabbath than in celebrating his miraculous cure (John 5:9–12)! But Jesus had not forgotten, nor did he disregard those gathered at the Bethesda Pools (John 5:3–6). The Redeemer had come to bring God's Kingdom and to seek and save the lost, not ignore them (Luke 19:10). Here at the Bethesda Pools, he showed his healing power and the hope of abundant life. Those at the pool may have been marginalized by the Temple aristocracy, but they were welcome in the Kingdom of God. Jesus healed the disabled man at the Bethesda Pools in the shadow of the Temple to offer them an invitation to his Kingdom.

JESUS TRAVELS TO THE TEMPLE FOR THE FEAST OF TABERNACLES

JOHN 7:1–38

Jesus had been chided by those who wanted him to leave Galilee and travel to Jerusalem for the Feast of Tabernacles to perform miracles and show himself to the world (John 7:2–4). Jesus answered, "You go to the Feast. I am not yet going up to this Feast, because for me the right time has not yet come" (John 7:8). After his critics left for Jerusalem, however, the right time came for Jesus to make the journey in secret. Clearly there was something important drawing Jesus to the Temple at this time—an opportunity he did not want to miss.

The Feast of Tabernacles had two primary purposes. First, because the feast fell in autumn at the close of the summer harvest season, it was the occasion for the nation of Israel to give thanks, celebrating the close of another successful agricultural year. Moses had instructed the people, "For seven days celebrate the Feast to the LORD your God at the place the LORD will choose" (Deut. 16:15). Second, this feast taught and reminded the people of an important history lesson. It reviewed the time Israel had spent in the wilderness under God's protecting hand as they traveled from Egypt to the Promised Land (Lev. 23:43).

There were three elements that helped accomplish the purposes of the festival. First, special offerings were made each day at the Temple in thanksgiving for the blessing

Pilgrims at the western wall of the Temple, celebrating the Feast of Tabernacles and holding the citron and *lulab*.

Fourth-century mosaic of the citron and *lulab*, symbols of the Feast of Tabernacles.

of the harvest (Lev. 23:36). Second, temporary shelters (also called booths or tabernacles) were built by families because God had directed the Israelites to live in these shelters during this special week as a reminder of how their ancestors lived during their stay in the wilderness (Lev. 23:42–43). Third, everyone had in hand a citrus fruit and a *lulab*, which was a cluster of three branches (Lev. 23:40)—such as myrtle, willow, and palm—that recalled the stages of the wilderness journey.[9]

For seven days during the feast the high priest descended to the Pool of Siloam with a golden pitcher, drew water, and returned through the Water Gate. The procession continued to the Great Altar, where this water was ceremonially poured into a funnel that led to the base of the altar.[10] Shaking the *lulab* in their hands, the Levites and the people then sang Psalms 113–118, praising God for blessings of the past and present.[11] Then the crowd quieted for a time of reflection, thinking about the Scriptures they had heard that week.

◀ Temple model—Water Gate (far right of the three gates at the base of the Temple). Jesus was probably standing near the Water Gate during the Feast of Tabernacles when he proclaimed, "If anyone is thirsty, let him come to me and drink" (John 7:37). © Dr. James C. Martin. Reproduction of the City of Jerusalem at the time of the Second Temple. (See full credit on page 4.)

They contemplated the words of Zechariah 9–14 that predicted the days of the Messiah. "On that day living water will flow out from Jerusalem" (Zech. 14:8).

On the last day, just one voice dared interrupt this ceremony. As Jesus speaks, we find the reason he had come to the Feast of Tabernacles at Jerusalem. "Jesus stood and said in a loud voice, 'If anyone is thirsty, let him come to me and drink. Whoever believes in me, as the Scripture has said, streams of living water will flow from within him'" (John 7:37–38; see also Isa. 44:3; 55:1).

A *sukkah* (Hebrew for "tabernacle"). Jewish families live in a *sukkah* during the Feast of Tabernacles (Hebrew, *sukkot*).

JESUS'S IDENTITY QUESTIONED IN JERUSALEM

JOHN 7:40–53

The discussion of Jesus's identity is the heart of John 7. Jesus had come to Jerusalem for the Feast of Tabernacles, and while there he spoke of his legitimacy and authority with increasingly clear language before large crowds. He said such things as, "I know him because I am of him and he sent me" (John 7:29; see also John 5:24). John's Gospel mentions two very different groups, the people of the land (Hebrew, *ha-am ha-aretz*) and the religious leaders, each of whom questioned how Jesus's messianic claims could coincide with his Galilean background.

The people of the land from Judea were divided as to Jesus's identity. Some recognized him to be a prophet and the Messiah (Deut. 18:15–19; John 5:45–47; 7:40–41), while others questioned his identity due to his Galilean background, asking a very important question: "How can the Christ come from Galilee? Does not the Scripture say that the Christ will come from David's family and from Bethlehem, the town where David lived?" (John 7:41–42).[12]

The religious leaders in Jerusalem mocked and cursed the people of the land for their ignorance of the Torah

Jerusalem (aerial view looking northeast).

(John 7:49). In this situation, however, some of the people of the land demonstrated a deeper understanding of God's promises. They knew the prophecy of Micah (Mic. 5:2) that pointed to Bethlehem as the place where the Messiah would be born (John 7:42). But others ignored that fact and viewed Jesus only as a Galilean from Nazareth.[13]

The Temple leadership had a bigger problem to overcome—it too was related to Jesus's Galilean connection. With the exception of those like Nicodemus, the religious leaders of Jerusalem rejected the claims Jesus and others made regarding his identity. They were not even willing to extend a hearing to Jesus in order to inquire more carefully into the matter—a hearing that their own law required (John 7:50–51). When Nicodemus raised this issue, the prejudice of these religious leaders against Galileans became obvious: "Are you from Galilee, too? Look into it, and you will find that a prophet does not come out of Galilee" (John 7:52).

There were a number of reasons why those in Judea generally held Galileans in contempt.[14] This region had historically been more open to Gentile invasion and influence and so was known as "Galilee of the Gentiles" (Matt. 4:15). Moreover, at this point, fewer priests lived

Galilean farmers working in the field in the early 1900s. The *ha-am ha-aretz* (Hebrew for "the people of the land") were farmers of the land.

in the Galilee region, so its residents were less likely to come to the Temple for all the required pilgrimages due to its distance. As a result, those in Galilee were viewed as less committed to the laws that were taught by the Temple leadership.[15] Discarding the contributions of Jonah, who was from the Galilean village of Gath Hepher (2 Kings 14:25; Jonah 1–4), three and a half miles from Nazareth, many Temple leaders mistakenly concluded that a prophet of value could not come from such a place. So certain religious leaders and people of the day would not accept Jesus's true identity because of his Galilean connections and their own ignorance or unwillingness.

Praying at the western wall of the Temple Mount.

Hill above Bethsaida in Galilee, the possible location of the feeding of the 5,000, where the people wanted to make Jesus king.

JESUS SENDS A BLIND MAN TO THE POOL OF SILOAM

JOHN 9

The question of Jesus's messianic legitimacy and authority raised in the seventh chapter of John progressed in the eighth and ninth chapters as inquiries by the Temple leadership continued and became increasingly barbed the longer Jesus remained in Jerusalem. In their efforts to discredit him, the Temple Pharisees brought a woman who had been caught in the act of adultery and chided Jesus to rule on her guilt (John 8:2–11).[16] This was followed by a series of confrontations in which Jesus clearly revealed his messianic legitimacy and authority, but certain Pharisees did not want to believe (John 8–9). One of those confrontations occurred when Jesus healed a man born blind.

Jesus was walking with his disciples in the vicinity of the Temple when they came upon a blind man. The disciples asked Jesus, "Rabbi, who sinned, this man or his parents, that he was born blind?" (John 9:2). The disciples' question exposed a common misconception among many that physical disabilities were the result of a person's or a parent's sinfulness.[17] Jesus quickly dismissed their question by answering, "Neither this man nor his parents sinned, . . . but this happened so that the work of God might be displayed in his life" (John 9:3). Then, giving testimony to his own messianic authority, Jesus mixed saliva and soil, placed it on the man's eyes, and told him to go and wash the mixture off in the Pool of Siloam (John 9:7).

The pool, located at the southern end of Jerusalem, was a public venue where people came to get water. As Jesus sent the man there to be healed, God's work was on full display, just as Jesus intended (John 9:8–9). After washing his eyes according to Jesus's instructions, the man could see.

When the Temple Pharisees learned of the healing, they had the man brought to them and heatedly challenged his story. Then these religious leaders intensely interrogated him and his parents, challenging them to explain how it was that he could now see after being born blind. The healed man's humble reply was simply, "I was blind and now I see! . . . If this man [Jesus] were not from God, he could do nothing" (John 9:25, 33).

Jesus's healing of this blind beggar pushed the Temple leadership into panic. Who was this man who could bring sight to a person born blind? The public testimony of the healed beggar that he now miraculously had his vision established Jesus's authenticity to those who were still wondering if the Messiah had arrived in Jerusalem.

Remains of the original roadway leading from the Temple Mount down to the Siloam Pool.

This testimony came from a man who had been a beggar, not from Jerusalem's educated religious leaders who were blinded by their own elitism and misguided traditions of men. By sending the blind man to the Pool of Siloam for healing, Jesus demonstrated to everyone in Jerusalem that the Son of Man was, in fact, in their midst regardless of whether or not they wanted to see him.

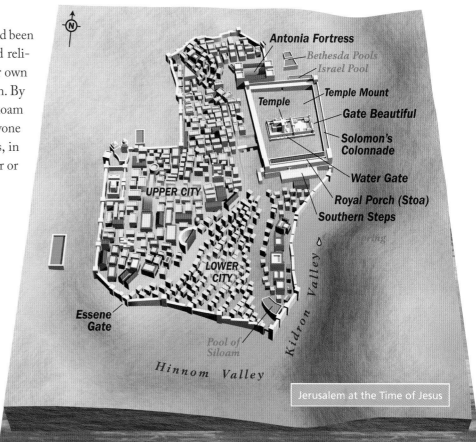

Jerusalem at the Time of Jesus

Antonia Fortress
Bethesda Pools
Israel Pool
Temple Mount
Temple
Gate Beautiful
Solomon's Colonnade
Water Gate
Royal Porch (Stoa)
Southern Steps
UPPER CITY
LOWER CITY
Essene Gate
Pool of Siloam
Kidron Valley
Hinnom Valley

Excavations of the Pool of Siloam.

THE FATHER'S SON IN SOLOMON'S COLONNADE

JOHN 10:22–30

John's Gospel also records what occurred when Jesus was in Solomon's Colonnade during the Feast of Dedication. We will see why Jesus chose that location and that time to repeatedly declare himself to be the Father's Son.

Although the name of King Solomon became associated with this open porch, it was part of a later renovation to the Temple complex made by Herod the Great.[18] He improved the site by creating a platform around the Temple that could hold more people. Herod then surrounded this platform with covered porches, each consisting of a roof held up by rows of marble columns.[19] The porch in which Jesus was walking during this exchange with the Jewish leaders was on the east side of the Temple and was called Solomon's Colonnade.

This was at the time of the celebration of the Feast of Dedication (John 10:22),[20] which is a Jewish festival that originated about 167 BC. Antiochus IV (Epiphanes) was a Greek king who had come to control the Promised Land and who attempted to destroy Judaism by incorporating Greek culture into Jewish society. Because the Temple played such an important role in maintaining the distinctiveness of the Jews, he set about defiling its altar and sanctuary (1 Macc. 1:36–61). A Jewish resistance was organized against this foreign intrusion and sought not just political freedom but religious restoration as well. When Judas Maccabaeus regained control of Jerusalem, he directed a complete and thorough cleansing of the sanctuary and restoration of Temple services (1 Macc. 4:36–58; 2 Macc. 10:1–8). In 164 BC on Chislev 25, smoke from sacrifices began

Architectural seam on the southern section of the Temple Mount's eastern wall. In Gospel times, it was believed that the stones on the right side were from the time of Solomon, thus the name Solomon's Portico. However, the stones actually date back only to the second century BC.

Jerusalem model—the inside of Solomon's portico.

© Dr. James C. Martin. Reproduction of the City of Jerusalem at the time of the Second Temple. (See full credit on page 4.)

to rise once again from this restored sanctuary. In commemoration of this rededication, the Jews commenced an annual eight-day celebration called the Feast of Dedication.

Thus there was a festive note in the air with people recalling the great restoration of the Temple during the days of the Maccabees. But by the time of the Gospels, the Temple had again been corrupted. Some of those in charge could not see the Messiah, even though he stood right before their eyes and proclaimed his identity as the Good Shepherd, with the power to give eternal life to his sheep (John 10:28). Here, as David and Isaiah had accurately prophesied, was the Son of God who was born to restore the flock to true worship in a way that Judas Maccabaeus could not (Pss. 16:8–11; 110:1; Isa. 7:14; Matt. 1:20–23; Acts 2:25–35).[21]

During the feast, as Jesus walked in Solomon's Colonnade, located along the eastern wall of the Temple Mount, the religious leaders insisted, "If you are the Christ, tell us plainly" (John 10:24). Of course Jesus had already done so many times in many ways. Nevertheless, he responded once again, boldly declaring in John 10:25–38 his association with the Father: "I and the Father are one" (John 10:30), and "Believe the miracles, that you may know and understand that the Father is in me, and I in the Father" (John 10:38). In doing so, Jesus demonstrated that it was not his failure to speak plainly about his identity but rather their unbelief that was the issue.

◀ Looking west from the Mount of Olives toward the outer eastern wall of the Temple Mount (i.e., the outer wall of Solomon's Portico).

Remnants of early architecture inside the eastern wall of the Temple Mount in the area of Solomon's Portico.

© Garo Nalbandian.

JESUS MEETS BARTIMAEUS ON THE JERUSALEM-JERICHO ROAD

MARK 10:46–52

Several months after the Feast of Dedication, Jesus raised Lazarus from the dead. The Temple leaders were so threatened by this miracle that they sought to arrest Jesus. So he took his disciples to the village of Ephraim until the initial threat had passed (John 11:1–57). We next find Jesus and his disciples coming into Jericho on their way to Jerusalem for Passover. It was then that Jesus had an important encounter with the blind man Bartimaeus.

Mark is not the only Gospel writer to recount the meeting between Jesus and Bartimaeus on the Jerusalem-Jericho road. But Mark clearly had a special interest in this exchange, not so much because of what Jesus did but because of what Bartimaeus said. To be sure, this was yet another compassionate miracle performed by Jesus, and it offers Mark's readers something unique as well. We will see what that contribution is and why it finds new meaning on the road that links Jericho with Jerusalem.

View looking west from the Jericho road toward the Cypros fortress. It was on the Jericho road that Jesus met blind Bartimaeus.

Blind man requesting donations.

Both Jesus and Bartimaeus made use of this road, but for very different reasons. Jesus left Jericho with Jerusalem as his destination. This trip took him through some of the most rugged and hostile terrain in the Promised Land, but even though it was difficult to travel, the Roman road was the most accessible way through the Judean Wilderness.[22] Bartimaeus came to this roadway for a different reason—not to travel but to beg. Bartimaeus lived on the margins of society and relied on the charity of others. His need stands in striking contrast to the lavish wealth of Jericho in the first century.[23] Thus Jesus and Bartimaeus both came to the Roman road, but for very different reasons.

As the two met, the exchange that occurred between them was significant. Bartimaeus pleaded for help and received it. He had hoped to receive a contribution that might make a minor change; instead he received a gift that revolutionized his life—Jesus restored his sight. What is also striking is what Bartimaeus gave to Jesus by addressing him as the Son of David. This was a very important detail. Not only did Bartimaeus shout this title, but he shouted it repeatedly (Mark 10:46–48). The title is important because it links Jesus to the messianic prophecies of Scripture such as Isaiah's: "A shoot will come up from the stump of Jesse; from his roots a Branch will bear fruit. The Spirit of the LORD will rest on him. . . . He will not judge by what he sees with his eyes, or decide by what he hears with his ears" (Isa. 11:1–3; see also Jer. 23:5–6; Ezek. 34:23–24). In this

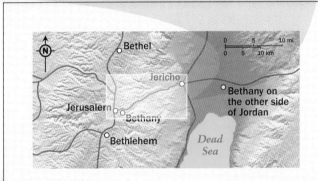

The Jerusalem-Jericho Road and New Testament Jericho

repeated phrase, Bartimaeus reminds us where Jesus was heading (Mark 10:32–34). Jesus, the King of Kings, was on his way to Jerusalem to rightfully claim David's throne. So it was on the road out of Jericho leading to Jerusalem that Bartimaeus addressed Jesus with a title that proclaimed his purpose for going to Jerusalem.

Jericho road (view looking east). Jesus and his disciples took this road up to Jerusalem after leaving Jericho.

JESUS STAYS IN THE HOUSE OF A "SINNER"

LUKE 19:1–10

While Jesus was passing through Jericho on his way to Jerusalem for Passover just prior to his crucifixion, a great crowd had gathered to see him. This included a tax collector by the name of Zacchaeus, in whose home Jesus said he "must [Greek, *dei*] stay" (Luke 19:5).

Zacchaeus was the chief tax collector in the region (Luke 19:2), which meant that although he was a Jew, Zacchaeus had become part of the Roman tax machinery. During the first century, Rome occupied and controlled the Promised Land, collecting a variety of taxes in the process.[24] The actual collection was accomplished by locals like Zacchaeus who pledged their support to the Roman effort and promised to deliver the appropriate

tax for their district. For their trouble, tax collectors were allowed to add a commission to the amount due.[25] So we find Zacchaeus, a chief tax collector, involved in keeping an eye on the income derived from the lucrative agricultural and commerce industry that passed through the Jericho area.[26]

The professional life of Zacchaeus had made him powerful at the expense of being viewed as a traitor by the people of the land. Because tax collectors were associated with the hated Roman occupation and because dishonesty and abuse of power was so closely allied with the tax collection process, this profession was counted among the despised trades.[27] The stigma

View looking west from Herod's northern palace toward the Cypros fortress.

Mosaic of the *Wedding of Dionysus and Ariadne*. Scenes similar to this would have been seen in homes of Hellenized Jews.

that clung to this occupation had even been used as an example in Jesus's earlier teaching about love: "If you love those who love you, what reward will you get? Are not even the tax collectors doing that?" (Matt. 5:46).

As Jesus passed through Jericho, there was a crowd around him. On his way, he looked up into a sycamore-fig tree, and called to the short man above him, "Zacchaeus, come down immediately. I must stay at your house today" (Luke 19:5). The disciples must have cringed as others in the crowd muttered, "He has gone to be the guest of a 'sinner'" (Luke 19:7). Of all the places he could have gone, why did he go to the home of Zacchaeus?

Jesus stayed at the home of Zacchaeus because there was something different about this tax collector, and his visit affirmed that difference. Luke tells us that Zacchaeus "ran" and "climbed a sycamore-fig tree" (Luke 19:4) in order to see Jesus.[28] When these actions are combined with his words promising to give half his possessions to the poor and to pay back four times the amount to any he might have cheated (Luke 19:8), we can appreciate why it was necessary for Jesus to be a guest in this man's home. He wanted Zacchaeus and all those who observed this event to know that even tax collectors could become members of his Kingdom;

the unthinkable was possible in the Kingdom of God. "Today salvation has come to this house, because this man, too, is a son of Abraham. For the Son of Man came to seek and to save what was lost" (Luke 19:9–10).

Jericho bath (pool complex), an example of Jericho's lavish homes and palatial estates.

◄ Sarcophagus scene (fourth century) of Zacchaeus climbing a sycamore tree to see Jesus.

PART 6

JESUS FACES THE CROSS

View from the Mount of Olives (Dominus Flevit Church), looking west toward Jerusalem.

As in part 5, we continue tracing the footsteps of Jesus in the environs of Jerusalem. But there is a change in tone as we approach Jesus's final week before his crucifixion. This time is marked by sharpened exchanges between Jesus and the corrupt leaders of the Temple who were searching for ways to kill him. Through this time of heightened tension, we again see how Jesus's actions and words take on new meaning when we consider the location. In that light, we will visit villages near Jerusalem—Bethany and Bethpage—and we will walk the roadway that connects these villages with Jerusalem. Finally, we will follow Jesus into the various courts of the Temple complex during the week that led to his crucifixion.

We will begin in Bethany, the village that witnessed the raising of Lazarus. A miracle of such magnitude in this village so close to Jerusalem threatened the Temple aristocracy to the extent that they decided, once and for all, to rid themselves of Jesus. Bethany was also the setting where one of his followers, Mary, poured perfume on the feet of Jesus. In revisiting the times when the Gospel writers have taken us to this place, we will come to understand the significance of Mary's actions.

We will also spend a moment in Bethpage, the village that provided the donkey for Jesus's entry into Jerusalem. Jesus's act of riding draws attention to the event and helps us to see how getting on a donkey at Bethpage continued to reveal the identity of Jesus as the Messiah.

From Bethany and Bethpage we will turn our attention to the roadway that connected them to Jerusalem. It was on this road that Jesus rebuked a fig tree and nearby atop the Mount of Olives that he prophesied of things to come—a discourse on the end times.

Then we come to the Temple complex itself. We will see that three men—Caiaphas, Pontius Pilate, and Jesus—all had a vested interest in the Temple complex, but interests that differed markedly from one another. It was those divergent interests that brought Jesus to the cross. We will listen in as Jesus offers an answer to the question about paying taxes to Rome. That question was shaped in order to entrap Jesus and bring him under suspicion of the Romans. Jesus's answer to the question of paying taxes to Rome revealed the hypocrisy of those who asked.

Also, we will travel with Jesus into the Court of Women where the offering boxes for the Temple were kept. Here we encounter a woman whose sacrificial act of giving displayed the sincerity of her faith. As Jesus faced the cross, all these events happened where they did for a reason.

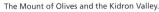

The Mount of Olives and the Kidron Valley.

Mosaic of Lazarus on the facade of the Church of Lazarus in Bethany.

Ossuary of the high priest Caiaphas.

To Joppa

To Bethlehem

Hinnom Valley

Kidron Valley

To Jericho

Church of Bethpage (bottom), with a
view looking northwest toward the
Church of the Ascension tower (top).

Olives

Bethpage

Mount of

Bethany

The village of Bethany in 1905.

A THREAT ERUPTS IN BETHANY

JOHN 11:1–53

Jesus had raised the dead before, but those stunning miracles had always occurred in the Galilee. He raised the widow's son at Nain (Luke 7:11–17) and Jairus's daughter in Capernaum (Luke 8:40–56). Yet neither of those Galilean miracles solicited such a hostile response from the religious leaders in Jerusalem as did the raising of Lazarus. As a result, the chief priests and certain Pharisees convened a meeting of the Sanhedrin, lamented the problems they thought this miracle would cause for them, and plotted to kill him (John 11:45–53). This hostile response from the religious leaders took shape because Jesus raised Lazarus, who had been dead for four days, near Jerusalem in Bethany of Judea.

Rome controlled the Promised Land by force, using a Roman governor and the weapons of the Roman soldiers to sustain their domination. Romans permitted Israel's supreme court, known as the Sanhedrin, to exist, but only under their subjection. The members of this court were predominantly from the priestly aristocracy who

Aerial view of Capernaum (view looking west), where Jesus raised Jairus's daughter.

were appointed to their legal position by Rome, but the court also included some leaders from the Pharisees and men of power[1] whose wealth had won them their standing. The balance of power

Scene of the raising of Lazarus, inside the church at Bethany.

Tomb of Lazarus.

was delicate, and numerous Sanhedrin leaders feared that Jesus's raising of Lazarus would be a catalyst for a revolt as the multitudes flocked to Jesus, causing Rome to curtail their authority. This is something they would not tolerate, as John's Gospel records, "Then the chief priests and the Pharisees called a meeting of the Sanhedrin. 'What are we accomplishing?' they asked. 'Here is this man performing many miraculous signs. If we let him [Jesus] go on like this, everyone will believe in him, and then the Romans will come and take away both our place and our nation'" (John 11:47–48).

The raising of Lazarus created this response because of the nature of the miracle and its location. When Jesus arrived at the tomb of Lazarus, Lazarus had already been dead for four days (John 11:17). This is an important detail, for according to the Pharisees a sufficient amount of time had to have passed since Lazarus died for them to agree that his corpse had started to decay. So it was without question that when Jesus performed this miracle, the decay of Lazarus's body was well under way.[2] This fact caused some of those Temple Pharisees who had earlier questioned Jesus's claims to now put their faith in him.

Only when we link this incredible miracle to its location can we fully grasp the significance of the Sanhedrin's response. It happened in close proximity to Jerusalem—Bethany was less than two miles away (John 11:18). Therefore the accessibility to the location of this miracle meant an increasing number of people would believe and follow the Messiah Jesus (John 12:11).

Since the Messiah was to inaugurate true worship in the Temple, the chief priests were particularly concerned that Jesus's ever-growing popularity would result in a riot leading to the loss of their power. So it was that the raising of Lazarus in Bethany four days after his death caused certain Sanhedrin members to meet in emergency session to consider the risk Jesus posed and to plot how to kill him.

◀ Village of Nain, where Jesus raised the widow's son.

MARY ANOINTS JESUS'S FEET IN BETHANY

JOHN 12:1–8

Although Jesus may have visited Bethany in Judea several times, only three visits are recorded in the Gospels: Luke 10:38–42; John 11:1–44; 12:1–11. According to Luke 10:38, Martha had a home in Bethany with her sister and brother, Mary and Lazarus. In looking at the three recorded visits, we will focus our attention on the behavior and actions of Mary in order to understand why she anointed Jesus's feet at an event where the family was gathered.

Luke recorded that Martha had opened her home to Jesus (Luke 10:38), and Mary sat at his feet, listening as he taught (Luke 10:39). There was plenty to do, and Mary's time with Jesus meant that Martha was left to do all of the work herself. In response to Martha's request that Jesus send Mary to help, he declared, "Only one thing is needed. Mary has chosen what is better, and it will not be taken away from her" (Luke 10:42). As we will see, it never was.

In the second recorded visit to Bethany (John 11:1–45), we find Mary grieving. Her brother, Lazarus, had died, and his body was in decay. Mary, who had sought the words of life from Jesus in Bethany, was now filled with sadness and was accompanied by those who had gathered at her house to comfort her (John 11:20, 31). So when Jesus entered Bethany after the death of Lazarus, Mary fell at his feet

Church and village remains of Bethany (view looking west).

Alabaster jars such as this one could be used to store valuable perfumes, oils, or ointments.

© Dr. James C. Martin. Elephantine Museum. Photographed by permission.

and said, "Lord, if you had been here, my brother would not have died" (John 11:32). Jesus wept and then proceeded to do the unimaginable by bringing Lazarus back to life (John 11:35–44).

The final recorded visit occurred six days before Passover (John 12:1). Sadness had given way to celebration. Jesus had raised Lazarus from the dead and restored him to his family. The man who had lain in a grave was reclining with family and friends at the dinner held in Jesus's honor (John 12:2). Then Mary, again, came to the feet of Jesus. This time she broke open a container of expensive perfume, poured it on Jesus's feet, and wiped his feet with her hair (John 12:3). When Judas and others objected to her actions (Matt. 26:8; Mark 14:4), Jesus defended her and redirected the attention of everyone in the room. "Leave her alone. . . . It was intended that she should save this perfume for the day of my burial" (John 12:7).

Portrayal of Mary anointing the feet of Jesus.

During this dinner in Jesus's honor, Mary, who had previously listened so attentively at Jesus's feet, now focused on what some of the others may have forgotten—the imminent death of the Savior of the world. Jesus had arrived in Bethany just six days before he was to be crucified (John 12:1).[3] With her actions of worship and honor of the Messiah, Mary helped redirect the attention of all present to what lay ahead for "the Lamb of God, who takes away the sin of the world" (John 1:29), the one who is the "resurrection and the life" (John 11:25).

The dome of the Dominus Flevit Church on the Mount of Olives is in the shape of a teardrop with a replica of a vase on each corner, to remind us of Jesus weeping over Jerusalem and Mary pouring out the symbol of her grief on Jesus's feet.

Mosaic of Mary and Martha with Jesus inside the Church of Lazarus in Bethany.

JESUS GETS ON A DONKEY AT BETHPAGE

MATTHEW 21:1–7

The Gospel writers document the travels of Jesus that literally crisscrossed hundreds of miles, yet only once do we specifically hear about him riding on a donkey. A week before Passover he got on a donkey at Bethpage, the city limits of Jerusalem. This unique act set in motion the events Jesus encountered during Passover week.

Two of Jesus's disciples were assigned the task to go ahead into the village of Bethpage and obtain a donkey. Jesus told them, "Go to the village ahead of you, and at once you will find a donkey tied there, with her colt by her. Untie them and bring them to me" (Matt. 21:2). Of course Jesus knew that this was going to cause a commotion, so he told the men how to respond to the objections that would arise. "If anyone says anything to you, tell him that the Lord needs them, and he will send them right away" (Matt. 21:3).

For those familiar with the topography of this area, the next detail of this event is unexpected. Jesus had left

The church at Bethpage, built in remembrance of the site where Jesus mounted the donkey for his triumphal entry into Jerusalem.

Jesus sent the disciples to find a donkey with its colt tied next to a house at Bethpage.

The Mount of Olives, Bethpage, and Bethany (aerial view looking northeast).

Bethany and walked up a very steep hill for about twenty minutes before arriving in the vicinity of Bethpage. By that point he was close to starting the downhill portion of his journey. If Jesus were going to ride at all, then one might expect him to ride uphill and walk downhill rather than the other way around. Thus Jesus's action of getting on a donkey at Bethpage invites us to look for an explanation.

Why did Jesus get on the donkey at Bethpage? The Gospel writers provide our answer. A large crowd of Passover visitors heard Jesus had left Bethany and was on his way to Jerusalem, so they went to meet him. Many of those gathered had either witnessed or heard of Jesus raising Lazarus from the dead and were anxious to proclaim him King as he entered Jerusalem (John 12:12–19). When he arrived at the city limits, he got on a donkey in fulfillment of a prophecy made hundreds of years earlier by the prophet Zechariah. Speaking "the word of the LORD Almighty" (Zech. 8:18), Zechariah helped a subsequent generation of readers identify the Messiah when he came. Matthew states that Jesus entered Jerusalem riding on the back of a donkey in fulfillment of Zechariah's prophecy: "Rejoice greatly, O Daughter of Zion! Shout, daughter of Jerusalem! See, your king comes to you, righteous and having salvation, gentle and riding on a donkey, on a colt, the foal of a donkey" (Zech. 9:9; see also Matt. 21:4).

That is where Bethpage comes in.[4] According to Jewish literature, Bethpage was considered the city limits of Jerusalem. For example, according to the Mishnah, bread prepared for use in the Temple was considered to have been made in the city of Jerusalem if it were made in Bethpage.[5] So if Jesus was going to enter Jerusalem riding on a donkey and identify himself as the King of Zechariah's prophecy, he had to get on that animal at the city limits of Jerusalem. When he did so, the crowds thronging to meet Jesus got the message, and from that time on this event has marked the beginning of Jesus's triumphal entry into Jerusalem.

Painting of the triumphal entry in the Russian Church of the Ascension.

CAIAPHAS, PILATE, JESUS, AND THE TEMPLE

MATTHEW 21:15–16; LUKE 13:1; JOHN 2:18–22

The Temple in Jerusalem was a magnet for thousands of people, but not all were drawn to this sanctuary for the same reason. Here we explore how three men—Caiaphas, Pilate, and Jesus—had three very different reasons for coming to the Temple courts. It is these differences that caused a violent collision in the week prior to Jesus's crucifixion.

Caiaphas entered public office in AD 18 when he was appointed as high priest by the Roman authorities.[6] But for those who had waited for the dawning of God's Kingdom, this appointment was a disappointment and a sham. Only a son of Zadok, priest at the time of David and Solomon, could inherit this office;[7] Caiaphas lacked the necessary lineage. As a Roman political appointee, he saw the Temple as a very promising business opportunity. People flocked to this location because it offered them something even more precious than food and water. It was symbolic of their

Caesarea Maritima (view looking north), with Pilate's residence in the foreground and a hippodrome in the background.

pursuit of a relationship with their Creator. Through the Temple marketplace and other means, Caiaphas planned to build his fortune on the backs of these worshipers.

Pilate became the military governor of Judea (or *prefect* from the Latin *praefecus*) in AD 26, making him the fifth Roman appointee to hold that office since AD 6. That was the date the Romans had turned Judea into a Roman imperial province—a designation given to those regions that were deemed more likely to rebel against their overlords. Pilate also wanted to gain as much personal wealth from his appointment as he could. But that appointment would be short-lived if word got out that he had failed to suppress seditious elements. This is where Pilate's interest in the Temple came into play. He knew that if rebellion against Rome took shape, it would

Pilate inscription discovered at Caesarea Maritima. This first-century Latin inscription states that Pilate dedicated a temple in honor of the emperor Tiberius.

do so in the Temple courts. Consequently, he sought to control the Temple from the Antonia Fortress. This tall building located at the northwest corner of the Temple complex housed Roman soldiers who looked down into the Temple courtyard and kept a watchful eye out to stop any insurgencies. When trouble arose, they could be on the scene quickly—as they did in the time of Paul (Acts 21:30–36). The Romans further controlled the Temple by keeping the high priestly vestments in the fortress under lock and key.[8]

Jesus became a rabbi at about the same time that Pilate came into his office. At his baptism, the Father declared, "This is my Son, whom I love; with him I am well pleased" (Matt. 3:17; see also Isa. 11:2). Because his Father's house had been so horribly compromised by the interests of both Caiaphas and Pilate, Jesus focused on the Temple's original purposes (Ps. 40:6–8) by offering his life as the full and complete sacrifice for all sin (Heb. 9:11–12; 10:1–10). So it was that Caiaphas, Pilate, and Jesus each came to the Temple with different intentions that brought them into confrontation.

Illustration representing a high priest.

© Dr. James C. Martin. Illustration by Timothy Ladwig.

Aerial view looking north of the Mount of Olives and the Temple Mount.
Jesus entered Jerusalem from Bethany, located on the east side of the Mount of Olives.

A FIG TREE ON THE ROAD TO JERUSALEM

MATTHEW 21:18–22

In this event we join Jesus and his disciples after his triumphal entry into Jerusalem. They had spent the night in Bethany and were now returning to Jerusalem along the same roadway (Matt. 21:17–18). As they were walking, Jesus was hungry and saw a fig tree. Seeing the leaves on the tree, he went up to pick its fruit. But the fig tree had no fruit, so he rebuked the tree saying, "May you never bear fruit again!" (Matt. 21:19).

In the Promised Land, the Judean fig tree was a tree whose annual lifecycle was well attested to in Scripture: "During Solomon's lifetime Judah and Israel, from Dan to Beersheba, lived in safety, each man under his own vine and fig tree" (1 Kings 4:25). During Jerusalem's winter months, the fig tree is devoid of leaves and fruit, and its gray, curvy, and barren branches give it away as a fig tree. However, in late spring, small leaves begin to appear on the branches, signaling the appearance of preseason figs (Hebrew, *pagé*—pronounced "pa-geh").[9] When Jesus was on his way from Bethany to Jerusalem, he observed a fig tree from a distance that had leaves erupting from the branches (Mark 11:12–13). Jesus approached the tree looking for preseason figs, which normally accompany the growth of the fig leaves. However, this particular tree proved to be hypocritical. It had the signs of fruit (i.e., fig leaves), but it did not produce any of the normally expected preseason

Preseason fig known as a *pagé*.

Fig tree near Bethpage on the road to Jerusalem.

figs among its leaves. So Jesus declared the tree would never bear fruit again.

While walking the road between Bethany and Jerusalem, Jesus prepared his disciples for what was to come by demonstrating his power over the hypocrisy of the Temple leadership. Previous encounters between Jesus and the chief priests and teachers of the law had revealed major disagreements. Jerusalem's religious leaders were threatened not only by Jesus's ever-increasing popularity but also by his statements about the upcoming destruction of the Temple (Matt. 24:2; Mark 14:58) and about his relationship to God as his Father (John 8:16).

Earlier Jesus had used metaphors of fruit-producing plants to teach his followers how to identify those who truly belong to God's Kingdom. "Make a tree good and its fruit will be good, or make a tree bad and its fruit will be bad, for a tree is recognized by its fruit" (Matt. 12:33). Jesus's encounter with the barren fig tree teaches the same lesson. The Temple aristocracy was hypocritical. By their religious dress and power, they had all the outward symbols of "religious fruit," but they bore no fruit. Thus, as the disciples prepared to wade into the increasingly hostile encounters with Jerusalem's religious leaders, Jesus showed his disciples that this corrupt leadership would come to an end.

Dried figs.

Ripe figs.

TAXES IN THE TEMPLE COURTS

LUKE 20:20-26

Jesus never shied away from the tough questions of life, but some questions were purposely asked to discredit Jesus's reputation and get him into trouble with the Roman authorities. We will see that the question on taxes was carefully worded and posed to Jesus in the Temple courts for such reasons.

This question grew from the frustration of the chief priests, teachers of the law, and elders who had been derailed in their attempts to sidetrack the teaching of Jesus in the Temple. When they demanded that Jesus tell them who had authorized his teaching and actions, they found themselves the object of a parable that showcased their continual blindness to the Scriptures illuminating Jesus as the Messiah (Ps. 118:22; Luke 20:2, 9–19). This called for a change in tactics. Rather than confront Jesus directly, these corrupt religious leaders solicited the help of spies who pretended to deliver an honest question but whose intentions were to entrap Jesus into saying something that would put him at odds with the Roman governor (Luke 20:20).

Consequently, while Jesus was speaking to the crowds, these spies approached with their carefully worded question: "Is it right for us to pay taxes to Caesar or not?" (Luke 20:21). The Jews paid a variety of taxes to an

Temple model—view looking south from the Antonia Fortress toward the Temple.

© Dr. James C. Martin. Reproduction of the City of Jerusalem at the time of the Second Temple. (See full credit on page 4.)

Struthian Pools. The Roman military controlled the water for Temple use, which came from Struthian Pools located within the compound of the Antonia Fortress.

oppressive Roman government that sought to enrich itself at the expense of the people of the land they occupied.[10] Some twenty years earlier a man named Judas of Galilee characterized this taxation as "slavery" and led a popular revolt against Rome.[11] Although the revolt gained a strong following, it died with Judas of Galilee, who was executed for his efforts (Acts 5:37). The spies, therefore, attempted to trap Jesus into associating with Judas's position of decrying the corrupt Roman tax system.

It is important to notice not just what this question offered but where it was proposed. Jesus was in the Temple courts (Luke 20:1), which meant he was never far from the ears of a Roman soldier. Herod the Great had renovated the Antonia Fortress, which resided on the northwest corner of the Temple complex[12] and was the barracks for a cohort of Roman soldiers who could quickly descend into the Temple courts if any disruption arose there. Because it was Passover, the eyes and ears of the Roman soldiers were likely even closer than the Antonia. During the high festival of Passover, the Roman governors characteristically ordered the Roman soldiers to leave the Antonia and take up positions behind the columns that circled the perimeter of the Temple complex.[13]

The spies sent by the Temple leadership presumed that Jesus would seize this opportunity to deliver a statement that would result in a wildly popular appeal. But in doing so, he would have potentially instigated a revolt against Rome. Instead Jesus offered an answer that astonished the spies and averted a conflict with Rome. "Give to Caesar what is Caesar's, and to God what is God's" (Luke 20:25).

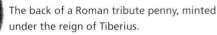

The back of a Roman tribute penny, minted under the reign of Tiberius.

© Dr. James C. Martin. The Rockefeller Museum, Jerusalem. Photographed by permission.

◄ Temple model. The Antonia Fortress (top right) was used by the Roman garrison to keep military control over the Temple.

© Dr. James C. Martin. Reproduction of the City of Jerusalem at the time of the Second Temple. (See full credit on page 4.)

A WIDOW'S GIFT AT THE TEMPLE TREASURY

LUKE 21:1–4

We do not know her name. So far as we can tell, she never exchanged a word with Jesus. Her entire story is related in less than seventy-five words, but in those words Jesus spoke of this generous woman as a shining example of faith. "I tell you the truth, . . . this poor widow has put in more than all the others. All these people gave their gifts out of their wealth; but she out of her poverty put in all she had to live on" (Luke 21:3–4). This happened in the Temple treasury, also known as the Court of Women.[14]

The Court of Women was the place where the faithful of God offered their coins in support of his Temple and for others in need of charity. Thirteen containers (Hebrew, *shopharoth*), each shaped like a long horn and each designated for a certain type of offering, were placed around this court to receive the coins.[15] Those offerings acknowledged God as the giver of all good gifts and provided a forum in which the contributor could declare trust in his promises, particularly his promise to provide the necessities of life.

Thus the widow's gift said something about her circumstances and her

Jerusalem model—the Court of Treasury, also know as the Court of Women (view looking southwest).

faith. Her very small gift was 100 percent of what she had to live on. During the time of the Gospels, the loss of a woman's spouse meant more than the loss of her life's mate; it also meant the loss of financial security, particularly when there was no son or family to help provide for her. A widow in such circumstances was almost certainly consigned to a life of poverty and was listed among the most

A shofar. Thirteen containers (Hebrew, *shopharoth*), each shaped like a long horn (shofar), were dispersed around the Court of Women.

Jerusalem model—Court of Women. The poor widow entered the Court of Women where the treasury containers were kept.

vulnerable members of society (Deut. 10:18; 24:17–22; 27:19).

The Lord had told Moses, when he was receiving offerings for the first tabernacle, that the gifts were to be received from those who wanted to give—those whose hearts prompted them (Exod. 25:2).[16] The apostle Paul echoed this sentiment when he said to the church at Corinth, "If the willingness is there, the gift is acceptable according to what one has, not according to what he does not have" (2 Cor. 8:12), for giving was to be a matter of the heart (2 Cor. 9:7).

The widow's gift in no way matched the size of the financial donations brought by the wealthy, but there was something special about her gift. The large offerings brought by others represented only a small percentage of what they had, so their donation did not represent much personal risk. This widow was already vulnerable, yet her heart was willing. She trusted God as she gave all the money she had. So there in the Temple treasury, Jesus commended her faith and her small gift when he said that she gave more than anyone else.

The lepton of Alexander Jannaeus is sometimes called the "widow's mite."

THE END TIMES, KIDRON VALLEY, AND THE MOUNT OF OLIVES

MATTHEW 24–25

*J*esus's discussion of the end times came a few days prior to his arrest and trials. The timing of this account is noteworthy, as well as the striking relationship to where it was presented—on the Mount of Olives above the Kidron Valley.

Passover was only a few days away (Matt. 26:1–2), which meant that Jesus's arrest and crucifixion were imminent. He warned everyone to be prepared for the upcoming destruction of the Temple and his subsequent return.

Jesus and the disciples were making what had become a familiar journey from Jerusalem to Bethany, where they would stay overnight. This meant they needed to cross the deep ravine of the Kidron Valley as well as travel over the Mount of Olives, which is a north-south

View looking west from the Mount of Olives toward the Temple Mount. Jesus took his disciples to the top of the Mount of Olives to discuss the end times.

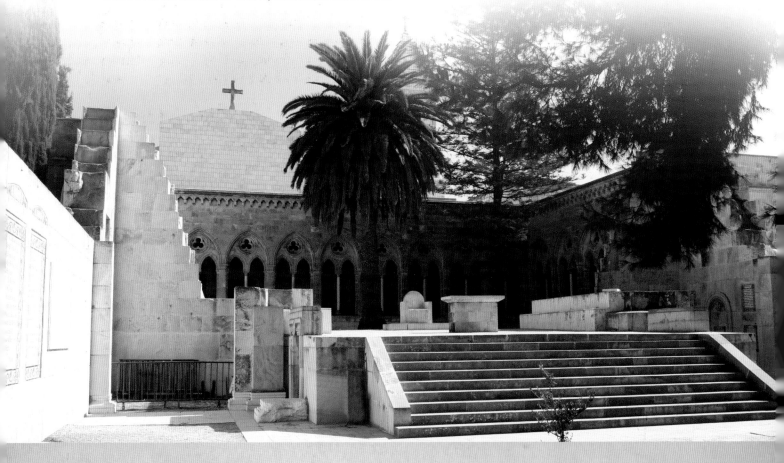

Cave under the fourth-century Byzantine Church of the Ascension, located on the southern end of the Mount of Olives.

ridge located on the east side of the Kidron Valley. It was on the Mount of Olives that the end-times discussion began. The disciples asked, "Tell us, . . . when will this happen, and what will be the sign of your coming and of the end of the age?" (Matt. 24:3).

The Kidron Valley and Mount of Olives were both associated in Scripture with judgment and the end of the age. For example, during the days of Israel's Divided Kingdom, the good kings of the Southern Kingdom brought Asherah poles, Baal cult objects, and pagan altars to the Kidron Valley along the western slopes of the Mount of Olives and destroyed them.[17] The Jewish historian Josephus reports that the evil queen of Judah, Athaliah, was executed in this valley.[18]

The return of the Son of Man is also a subject of Israel's prophets. In describing the return of the Son of Man, Zechariah says that day will be marked by the appearance of the Lord on the Mount of Olives (Zech. 14:4). Jesus refers to another prophet, Joel, who says that the sun will be darkened and the moon will not give its light (Joel 2:10, 31). Joel also speaks of the nations being judged in the Valley of Jehoshaphat (Joel 3:2, 11), which in Hebrew means "the Lord judges." This valley is identified throughout history as the Kidron Valley. "I will gather all nations and bring them down to the Valley of Jehoshaphat. There I will enter into judgment against them concerning my inheritance, my people Israel, for they scattered my people among the nations and divided up my land" (Joel 3:2).

Thus it was on the Mount of Olives overlooking the Kidron Valley, which was long associated with the judgment of idolatry and the coming day of the Lord, that Jesus offered his timely warning to his disciples to flee Judea when they saw the "abomination that causes desolation" (Dan. 9:27), for "there will be great distress . . . never to be equaled again" (Matt. 24:21).[19]

Judea Capta sestertius coin, minted by the Emperor Vespasian after the destruction of Jerusalem and the Temple, as predicted by Jesus.

© Dr. James C. Martin. The British Museum. Photographed by permission.

◀ Pater Noster Church, built on the Mount of Olives over the fourth-century Byzantine Church of the Ascension, commemorates where Jesus announced the upcoming destruction of the Temple.

PART 7

THE ARREST AND TRIALS OF JESUS

Johann Christian Braun's seventeenth-century ivory *Ecce Homo* ("Behold the Man").
© Dr. James C. Martin. Musée du Louvre;
Autorisation de photographer et de filmer—LOUVRE.

During the week of Passover in the days prior to his crucifixion, Jesus remained in Jerusalem. The Gospel writers bring various individuals to the forefront of their accounts, such as Peter, Judas, the corrupt religious leaders, Pontius Pilate, and Herod Antipas. As these people interacted with Jesus and others, it was not only what they said and did but also where these things took place that is critical to our understanding of the events surrounding the arrest and trials of Jesus.

Jesus met with the disciples in an upper room around a table specifically prepared for the celebration of Passover. This table provided an eating surface, but more important were the places for the participants that revealed something about each one's social importance. Upon examination, we will come to understand the significance of Peter's place at the table.

With the meal complete, Jesus and his disciples left for Gethsemane. From this industrial olive grove Jesus could plainly see the two paths before him: one leading to the Wilderness of Judea and away from his suffering; the other leading to Golgotha and the cross that would rescue the world. Jesus was committed to the path that led to the cross, and he was arrested. In that context we will explore why Peter used his knife to cut off the ear of the high priest's servant and then followed Jesus to the courtyard of the high priest.

In the Gospels, Judas remained mostly in the background until shortly before the crucifixion. His betrayal of Jesus earned him thirty silver coins. We will explore why he later threw those coins into the Temple complex and why the religious leaders used those coins to purchase the potter's field.

The betrayal of Jesus and his arrest led quickly to his trial before the Sanhedrin. Caiaphas concluded the Sanhedrin's investigation of Jesus and declared him to be worthy of death, so the chief priests led him to the Roman governor, Pontius Pilate. As the Jewish religious leaders approached the Gentile headquarters of Pilate, they watched their steps very carefully. They went as far as the courtyard but refused to enter Pilate's quarters for a reason.

From this point forward it is Pilate who commands much of our attention. At a place referred to as the "Stone Pavement" (John 19:13), the Roman imperial procurator, Pilate, conducted Jesus's trial. It was in this place that Pilate's political vulnerability became very clear. He delayed giving a verdict until such time as he could isolate himself from any political fallout resulting from Jesus's crucifixion. When he sent Jesus to Herod Antipas, king of Galilee, for judgment, Herod treated Jesus brutally but refused to take any legal action. We will see that by washing his hands at the judge's seat, Pilate mocked the chief priests by mimicking a Jewish ritual. From Passover table to the Roman judge's seat, we will see again and again that event and place come together in meaningful ways.

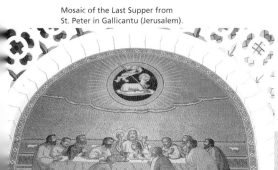

Mosaic of the Last Supper from St. Peter in Gallicantu (Jerusalem).

Church of All Nations (Gethsemane).

Tyrian shekels were probably used to pay Judas for his betrayal of Jesus.

© Dr. James C. Martin. Eretz Israel Museum, Tel Aviv, Israel. Photographed by permission.

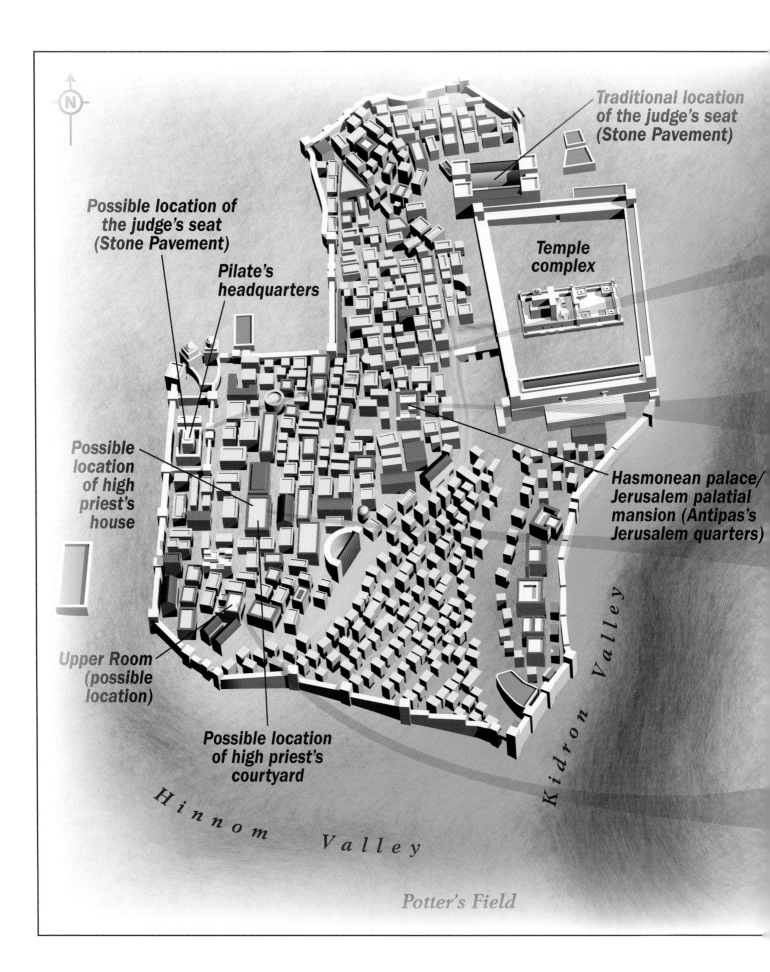

Traditional location of the judge's seat (Stone Pavement)

Possible location of the judge's seat (Stone Pavement)

Pilate's headquarters

Temple complex

Possible location of high priest's house

Hasmonean palace/ Jerusalem palatial mansion (Antipas's Jerusalem quarters)

Upper Room (possible location)

Possible location of high priest's courtyard

Kidron Valley

Hinnom Valley

Potter's Field

Possible locations of Gethsemane

Reconstructed towers on the site of Herod's palace in Jerusalem. This palace was later used by Pontius Pilate.

Model of Jerusalem's Hasmonean palace. Herod Antipas probably stayed at this complex when he came to Jerusalem.

© Dr. James C. Martin. Reproduction of the City of Jerusalem at the time of the Second Temple. (See full credit on page 4.)

Excavations of the priestly estates in Jerusalem.

© Dr. James C. Martin. The Wohl Archaeological Museum and Burnt House, Jerusalem.

Model of the complex where Jesus ate the Last Supper with his disciples.

© Dr. James C. Martin. Reproduction of the City of Jerusalem at the time of the Second Temple. (See full credit on page 4.)

PETER AT THE SERVANT'S SEAT

JOHN 13:2–17

Jesus had instructed Peter and John to go and prepare the Passover meal. After everything was in order, Jesus and the disciples reclined at the table (see Matt. 26:20; Mark 14:18; Luke 22:14; John 13:23), strongly suggesting that this Passover meal was eaten around a *triclinium*, a kind of table customarily used for special occasions such as Passover. The placement of each guest denoted a level of hierarchy from the most important person to the least important.[1]

Leonardo da Vinci's famous fifteenth-century mural known as "The Last Supper" depicts the disciples sitting at a European style table. The triclinium, however, was a low, three-sided surface at which the participants reclined on their left elbow and ate with their right hand.

Within the cultural context, Jesus was probably reclining in the host's position with John immediately to his right with his head against Jesus's chest (see John 13:23).[2] Judas would have been reclining to Jesus's left, facing Jesus's back. This can be deduced because Jesus dipped a piece of bread and gave it to Judas, indicating the two of them were in very close proximity (John 13:26).

© Dr. James C. Martin. Eretz Israel Museum, Tel Aviv, Israel. Photographed by permission.

When Jesus announced one of those at this table would betray him, Peter motioned across the table to John to ask Jesus whom he was referring to. This exchange of gestures is easily visualized when we see Peter in the designated location for the servant, directly across from John.[3] If this reconstruction is correct, then we might ask why Peter was in the servant's position.

Scene from a first-century sarcophagus of a person reclining.

© Dr. James C. Martin. Musée du Louvre; Autorisation de photographer et de filmer—LOUVRE.

Artistic rendition of the possible seating arrangements of the Last Supper (after Edersheim).

© Dr. James C. Martin. Illustration by Timothy Ladwig.

John Jesus Judas

X   X   X   X   X

                        X

                        X

                        X

X   X   X   X   X

Peter

Certainly Peter's close relationship with Jesus and apparent high standing among the disciples suggest there should have been a place of honor for him at the Passover table. Jesus had changed Simon's name to Peter (i.e., the rock) and had given him "the keys of the kingdom" several months earlier at Caesarea Philippi (Matt. 16:19; see vv. 17–19). The purpose of a rabbi was to make authoritative and binding definitions of the law, so that meant Peter was being elevated to the position of rabbi and had the ability to bind and loosen those definitions.[4]

With this in mind, we find that the most obvious indication that Peter was reclining in the servant's place came when Jesus began to wash the disciples' feet—an act that should have been performed by the one in the servant's position. But that person was not doing the job, so Jesus proceeded to do it himself. No one objected until Jesus came to Peter, who protested, "Lord, are you going to wash my feet? . . . No, . . . you shall never wash my feet" (John 13:6, 8). For whatever reason, Peter, as the one sitting in the servant's position, refused to carry out what should have been his task. Therefore, Jesus demonstrated the meaning of leadership not only to the recently appointed rabbi, Peter, but to all the disciples: "Now that I, your Lord and Teacher, have washed your feet, you also should wash one another's feet. I have set you an example that you should do as I have done for you" (John 13:14–15).

Remains of a triclinium table in a Roman military camp at Masada.

JESUS PRAYS IN GETHSEMANE

MATTHEW 26:36–46; LUKE 22:39–46

As they completed the Passover, Jesus and his disciples lifted their voices in a hymn (Mark 14:26) before retracing the familiar path to the Mount of Olives. They stopped at a place that had hosted this group on many other occasions—Gethsemane, an industrial olive grove located on the lower western slope of the Mount of Olives, which was adjacent to the Judean Wilderness. Jesus had often taken the disciples there to teach them and to pray (John 18:1–2). This time, however, was different because Jesus agonized in Gethsemane for a reason.

Jesus had decided before this night to lay down his life. "What shall I say? . . .

It was for this very reason I came to this hour" (John 12:27). Yet there is no mistaking the intensity and pain of this time before his arrest. Sorrowful and troubled, Jesus said to Peter, James, and John, "My soul is overwhelmed with sorrow to the point of death." Then he turned to his Father and prayed, "My Father, if it is possible, may this cup be taken from me. Yet not as I will, but as you will" (Matt. 26:38–39). Never before have we heard this kind of language come from the Savior's mouth, and never before have we seen him so filled with anguish that bloody sweat—a physiological condition known as hemohidrosis[5]—fell from his face to the ground (Luke 22:44). The name of this olive grove joins in describing the intensity of

Gethsemane olive trees dating back nearly 1,500 years. In the first century, Gethsemane (i.e., "the place of the olive press") was an industrial olive grove.

Mosaic of Jesus praying in Gethsemane, inside the Church of All Nations.

the moment; it was named after the industrial oil presses located within it (Hebrew, *gat*, meaning "press"; *shemen*, meaning "oil"). Jesus's agony was so intense that it was as if he were being pressed, squeezed, and crushed by the mechanical force of an olive press.

Looking west from Gethsemane, Jesus would have seen the stately outline of the Temple. Here over the ages thousands of animals had been slaughtered, their blood staining the altar. But this animal blood had no power on its own because it was merely a placeholder awaiting the day when God's Son would shed his blood as the ultimate sacrifice for sin. "But those sacrifices are an annual reminder of sins, because it is impossible for the blood of bulls and goats to take away sins. . . . 'Then I said, "Here I am—it is written about me in the scroll—I have come to do your will, O God"'" (Heb. 10:3–4, 7). The westward view from Gethsemane was a reminder of all that lay ahead—the Temple, the altar, the blood, and the abandoned rock quarry that would be used as a cemetery where Jesus's blood would be shed.

With eyes looking east from Gethsemane, Jesus, who was grief-stricken in prayer, was offered an alternative. Just over the ridge of the Mount of Olives, a forty-five-minute walk into the empty isolation of the Judean Wilderness offered a way of escape. The rugged canyons of the Judean Wilderness had frequently provided refuge to those looking for a safe haven from the hand of hostile authorities. King David found refuge in this wilderness from the vengeance of Saul. Now the Prince of

Peace—the one who was promised to reign from David's throne; the Counselor whose increase of government and peace would never end (Isa. 9:6–7)—could have traveled east to escape his imminent death. So it was at Gethsemane that two different directions offered two different paths for Jesus to take—one led to the wilderness and the other to the cross. Of his own accord, the Good Shepherd chose the path of laying down his life for his sheep (John 10:14–15; 18:11).

◀ The Church of All Nations, built over the area of the Garden of Gethsemane.

Germain Pilon artistic relief (AD 1582) of Christ in Gethsemane.

PETER CUTS OFF THE EAR OF THE HIGH PRIEST'S SERVANT

JOHN 18:2–11

After his time in prayer, Jesus turned resolutely to meet Judas, who was leading those coming to arrest him. As the detachment of soldiers and some Sanhedrin officials approached, Jesus identified himself and willingly surrendered. During the encounter, Peter drew his weapon (Greek, *macharia*, meaning "short sword" or "dagger") and cut off the right ear of the servant of the high priest. Here we will explore the reason Peter's action was so carefully directed at the ear of this particular man.

Peter's aggressive action is best explained by an exchange he had with Jesus a few hours earlier. When Jesus spoke directly and openly about the threatening hours ahead and his departure from this world (John 13:31–36), Peter boldly promised he would lay down his life for Jesus: "Lord, why can't I follow you now? I will lay down my life for you." In reply, Jesus questioned Peter's resolve: "Will you really lay down your life for me? I tell you the truth, before the rooster crows, you will disown me three times!" (John 13:37–38). Perhaps those

stinging words stayed with Peter so that when Jesus's opponents moved in to arrest him, Peter was quick to draw his weapon.

But why did he cut off the ear of the servant of the high priest? Given the way John's Gospel calls attention to this detail, it would be a mistake to presume that Peter randomly struck the ear. Peter was a fisherman whose skill in handling a knife was well honed, so we can assume that he cut his intended target. When we combine the ear and its

Scene of the arrest of Jesus, inside the Church of All Nations (Gethsemane).

owner together with history from the time of Herod the Great, we may come to understand why Peter directed his dagger at whom and where he did.

The servant of the high priest may have served as a Sanhedrin official who represented the high priest.[6] Josephus describes how the high priest used such a representative to carry out his business—particularly shady business like taking tithes directly from the threshing floor, by which the priestly aristocracy stole from the ordinary priests.[7] Thus an attack on the servant of the high priest was an attack on the high priest himself, designed to send a message to everyone how Peter felt about the one occupying that office.

Cutting off the ear may further be explained by historical precedence. In about 40 BC the Hasmonean leader Mattathias Antigonus rebelled against Herod

Coin of the high priest Mattathias Antigonus, with the symbol of the menorah.

© Dr. James C. Martin. Eretz Israel Museum, Tel Aviv, Israel. Photographed by permission.

the Great. When captured, Antigonus was brought before John Hyrcanus, the high priest whom Herod had appointed. Taking advantage of his proximity to the high priest, Antigonus leaned in and bit off the high priest's ear. Since Jewish law required that the high priest be free of physical deformities, Josephus explains this unusual action was an attempt to draw attention to the illegitimacy of the high priest.[8] So Peter's well-aimed strike on the ear of the representative of the high priest may well have been designed to send his own message about the corruption of the high priest, Caiaphas, who at that time filled the office.[9]

Painting from the Church of the Holy Sepulcher, depicting Peter cutting off the servant's ear.

◀ Short sword (Greek, *macharia*), from the first or second century.

© Dr. James C. Martin. Collection of the Israel Museum, Jerusalem, and courtesy of the Israel Antiquities Authority, exhibited at the Shrine of the Book, the Israel Museum, Jerusalem. Photographed by permission.

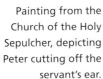

PETER'S DENIAL IN THE HIGH PRIEST'S COURTYARD

JOHN 18:12-27

Following the arrest of Jesus, he was first taken to the former high priest, Annas (John 18:13), and then sent on to the current high priest, Caiaphas. Peter and another disciple followed at a distance into the courtyard of the high priest. Of all the locations associated with the disciples' time in Jerusalem, this courtyard receives comparatively little attention and with good reason. Archaeologists thus far have not produced strong evidence to mark its precise location.[10] We suspect that Peter would have preferred that it remain as anonymous as possible because it represents a horrendous event in his life. He went to this courtyard in a bid to support Jesus, but the most

Jerusalem model. The red-roof buildings represent the palatial estates of the families of the priestly aristocracy.

significant memory associated with the place became his denial of Jesus.

Although the precise location of the high priest's courtyard at that time is unknown, it was probably either located in the affluent suburb of Jerusalem known as the Upper City or it was affiliated with the Temple complex.[11] Archaeologists have uncovered palatial homes in the Upper City of Jerusalem that provided luxurious living space and floor plans that included a central courtyard completely enclosed by the rooms of the wealthy estate.[12] Wherever it was located, the courtyard of the high priest was not open to the general public. When Peter arrived, he had to wait outside at the door while the other disciple, who was known to the high priest, entered. And it was only when that disciple secured the right for Peter to enter that access was granted (John 18:15–16).

Neither John nor any of the other Gospel writers directly state why Peter entered the

The Church of St. Peter in Gallicantu in Jerusalem commemorates Peter's denial of Jesus in the courtyard of the high priest.

Steps leading up to the palatial estates of the high priests.

courtyard. They simply acknowledge that at the time of Jesus's arrest, the disciples all scattered (Matt. 26:56), but Peter and another unnamed disciple quickly gathered themselves and followed Jesus to the courtyard of the high priest. Perhaps Peter had a special reason to be there; he had promised Jesus his unfailing support and willingness to die for him (John 13:37). Maybe he entered this courtyard in order to get as close to Jesus as possible. But this place in which Peter wanted to be loyal to Jesus became the place associated with his denial of the Master.

Jesus had told Peter that before the rooster crowed, he would engage in three acts of denial rather than loyalty (John 13:38). The *rooster crow* (i.e., *cock crow*) may be a reference to an actual rooster, but it is more likely a reference to the trumpet blast that signaled the beginning of the liturgical day at the Temple. This trumpet blast was called "cock crow."[13] While standing in the courtyard of the high priest, Peter was challenged three different times to associate himself with Jesus. On each occasion he denied his Lord. As he was speaking the words of the third denial, "cock crow" sounded, and Jesus turned and looked straight at Peter (Luke 22:60–62). Peter had come to this courtyard, risky though it was, in order to prove his loyalty to Jesus. Ironically, it became the place that marked his verbal denial.

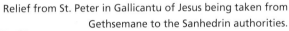

Relief from St. Peter in Gallicantu of Jesus being taken from Gethsemane to the Sanhedrin authorities.

JUDAS THROWS MONEY INTO THE TEMPLE

MATTHEW 26:14–16; 27:3–10

udas handed Jesus over to the Temple vanguard, people who were determined to have him killed—an act of betrayal that to this day has remained linked to his name. With the full weight of guilt and shame over what he had done, Judas attempted to return the money. But when the chief priests and certain elders showed no interest in his remorse, "Judas threw the money into the temple and left" (Matt. 27:5). Once again insight obtained from Jewish culture will show that he threw the money where he did for a reason.

Judas participated in the evening meal in Bethany given to honor Jesus (John 12:2). This meal became a reminder that the time of Jesus's death was near (Matt. 26:12). During this time, Judas set off to find the chief priests and offered to betray Jesus to them (Mark 14:10). His plan was to lead them to a place where they could arrest Jesus when the multitude of Jesus's followers would be unaware of the proceedings. An agreement was made, and Judas was given thirty silver coins (Matt. 26:14–16).

The actual arrest of Jesus was later set in motion when Judas departed from the upper room (John 13:30). After Jesus was taken into custody and condemned, Judas was seized with remorse. He found the chief priests who had paid him for his services and confessed his sin of betraying innocent blood. The chief priests, however, had what they wanted. Their sights were set not on justice but on the elimination of Jesus, so they refused to take back the money. At that moment Judas threw the money into the Temple courts.

This curious action may well be illuminated by a passage from the Mishnah that speaks about the selling of a home. Jewish tradition allowed the seller of a home to change his mind up to one year after the

Excavations inside the Huldah Gates. When Judas returned the money to the Sanhedrin leaders, he would have most likely entered the Temple courtyards through the Huldah Gates.

© Garo Nalbandian.

Greek inscription for a deed to a house.

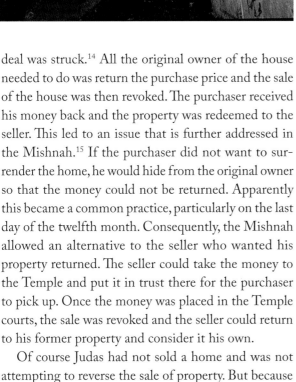

© Dr. James C. Martin. Thessalonica Museum. Photographed by permission.

deal was struck.[14] All the original owner of the house needed to do was return the purchase price and the sale of the house was then revoked. The purchaser received his money back and the property was redeemed to the seller. This led to an issue that is further addressed in the Mishnah.[15] If the purchaser did not want to surrender the home, he would hide from the original owner so that the money could not be returned. Apparently this became a common practice, particularly on the last day of the twelfth month. Consequently, the Mishnah allowed an alternative to the seller who wanted his property returned. The seller could take the money to the Temple and put it in trust there for the purchaser to pick up. Once the money was placed in the Temple courts, the sale was revoked and the seller could return to his former property and consider it his own.

Of course Judas had not sold a home and was not attempting to reverse the sale of property. But because guilt was overtaking him, Judas wanted out of the deal he had made with the chief priests. Perhaps this best explains why he threw the betrayal money into the Temple courts. Conceivably it was his effort to revoke the deal that had betrayed Jesus into the hands of those whose actions would bring about his death.[16]

◀ Jerusalem model—Huldah Gate entrances into the Temple complex.

THE PURCHASE
OF THE POTTER'S FIELD

MATTHEW 27:6–10

After Judas threw the thirty silver coins into the Temple, his life came to a tragic conclusion when he ended it himself. The one unresolved matter that lingered in connection with him was those coins—the money used to purchase the betrayal of Jesus. As we will see, those coins could not be used for improvements in the Temple or Temple service. Consequently, the chief priests used the money to purchase the potter's field.[17]

Typically the money placed in the Temple treasury was put to work in a variety of ways,[18] but there was a problem with the coins Judas had thrown into the Temple courts. Jewish tradition stated that any money that had been associated with a crime or was at all clouded with suspicion should be removed from the Temple treasury and put to work in some public project to benefit society, such as the development of a water system.[19] That is what happened with the thirty silver coins. "The chief priests picked up the coins and said, 'It is against the law to put this into the treasury, since it is blood money'" (Matt. 27:6). Instead they purchased the potter's field located outside the city walls.[20] This plot of ground was then set aside for

◀ Painting from the Monastery of Onesiphorus, depicting the hanging of Judas.

First-century tombs in the area of the potter's field.

the burial of foreigners who died in Jerusalem (Matt. 27:7).

As early as the fourth century, Christians pointed to a field at the southeastern end of the Hinnom Valley above the confluence with the Kidron Valley as the location of this potter's field. The location may well be associated with an earlier record that is supported, at least in part, by a passage in Jeremiah that speaks of the shedding of innocent blood (Jer. 19:1–4). The Lord directed Jeremiah to purchase a clay jar from a potter. To do so, the prophet exited through the Potsherd Gate and entered the Ben Hinnom Valley.[21] Perhaps this association with Jeremiah explains the reason for the name "potter's field."

When the chief priests took the thirty pieces of silver that Judas returned and purchased the potter's field, a link connected them to certain corrupt Temple leaders of an earlier time as mentioned by the prophet Zechariah. In Zechariah 11:12–13, the prophet mentions thirty pieces of silver that were thrown to the potter in the Temple in order to identify the religious leaders who

had rejected the God of Israel. "I am going to raise up a shepherd over the land who will not care for the lost, or seek the young, or heal the injured" (Zech. 11:16). This is an apt description of those who purchased the potter's field.

So it was literally within days of Judas's death and the purchase of this land that people stopped calling it the "potter's field" and began calling it *Akeldama*, which is Aramaic for "Field of Blood" (Acts 1:19). This name is a reminder of the true price of this field.

Cliff overlooking the Hinnom Valley (with the potter's field in the background)—the possible site where Judas hung himself.

◀ Aerial view looking southwest toward the Monastery of Onesiphorus, which commemorates the potter's field, also known as the "Field of Blood."

THE PROBLEM
WITH PILATE'S QUARTERS

JOHN 18:28

The goal of the corrupt Temple leadership had long been to disable the threat of the Messiah's immense popularity by eliminating him. When Jesus identified himself to his accusers as the Son of Man in direct fulfillment of Daniel's prophecy (Dan. 7:13–14), they mistakenly thought they had all the evidence needed to declare him guilty of blasphemy and worthy of death (Matt. 26:64–66). Due to political ramifications if a riot occurred, and because of religious issues related to the coming Passover, they sought action on this matter from the Roman governor, Pontius Pilate. With Jesus in custody, they set off for Pilate's headquarters. Upon arrival, they stopped short of entering for a reason.

We might expect Jesus's civil trial to be at Pontius Pilate's primary residence at Caesarea Maritima on the Mediterranean seacoast (Acts 23:33–24:1). Due to political tensions, however, the Roman governor had temporarily moved his headquarters to Jerusalem during Passover. While in the city, he stayed in the magnificent palace previously built and occupied by Herod the Great located on the northwest corner of the Upper City in Jerusalem.[22] This palace of Herod the Great, the one who had tried to kill Jesus as a child,

Model of Herod the Great's palace, which was later used as the Jerusalem palace for Roman governors such as Pilate.

became the setting for the trial that led to Jesus's execution as an adult.

Although the corrupt priestly families of Sadducees (referred to in John's Gospel as "the Jews") were determined to see this sentence carried out quickly, they could not defile themselves in the process.[23] Therefore, when they brought Jesus to Pilate's headquarters they

First-century stone cups. Stone vessels were often used for drinking, eating, and storage because, according to Jewish law, stone did not transmit impurities.

© Dr. James C. Martin. The Wohl Archaeological Museum and Burnt House, Jerusalem.

First-century Jerusalem sewer system. Jews during this period thought of Gentile homes as cemeteries and therefore considered them unclean, because the Romans placed the remains of aborted babies in their sewers.

© Dr. James C. Martin. The Wohl Archaeological Museum and Burnt House, Jerusalem.

went no farther than the courtyard "to avoid ceremonial uncleanness" (John 18:28). This uncleanness was not related to personal hygiene but to regulations that God had put in place for Israel centuries earlier. According to Leviticus 11–15, the experiences and objects of everyday life fell into two distinct categories: those that made one ceremonially unclean and those that did not. This requirement to remain ritually clean was particularly important for the priests, who not only ate the Passover meal with their families but also offered sacrifices on behalf of the people. Any defilement at this time prohibited them from making the Passover sacrifices.[24]

Therefore, the priests were very careful not to enter the domain of a Gentile, like Pilate, which would make them ritually unclean. Peter alluded to that when speaking to Gentiles: "You are well aware that it is against our law for a Jew to associate with a Gentile or visit him" (Acts 10:28). Interestingly, this uncleanness even clung to the garments that were kept in such a house. Josephus reports that the garments of the high priest were kept in the Antonia Fortress and had to be released seven days before the high festival of Passover so they could be ritually purified after being stored in that Gentile environment. Because all Gentile homes were considered unclean, Jewish law decreed that all who entered their homes became unclean. But what was true of the residence proper was not true of the courtyard.[25] Consequently, when Caiaphas and his Sadducee cohorts brought Jesus to Pilate, they could not enter the palace without becoming ritually defiled. Therefore they remained in the courtyard where Pilate had his various exchanges with them until he ordered Jesus to be crucified (John 19:13–16).

Ritual purification bath (Hebrew, *mikveh*). Jewish law required ritual purification for those who came into contact with anything deemed unclean.

PILATE SENDS JESUS TO HEROD ANTIPAS

LUKE 23:1–12

As Passover was approaching, the Roman governor, Pontius Pilate, was faced with a dilemma. The high priest, Caiaphas, had brought his entourage requesting that Pilate condemn Jesus to death. Under most circumstances Pilate would have been happy to oblige. This time, however, there was reason for closer scrutiny before carrying out the request, and after several encounters involving Caiaphas and Jesus, Pilate realized the full ramifications of Caiaphas's request. So when Pilate learned that Jesus was a Galilean and that some of his alleged crimes were committed in Galilee, he sent Jesus to Antipas (the son of Herod the Great).

Antipas was in Jerusalem at the time, and was most likely staying at the Hasmonean palace, located in the Upper City of Jerusalem just a short distance from the palace where Pilate was conducting the trial of Jesus (Luke 23:7). This palace had been built decades earlier by Jewish kings of the Hasmonean dynasty who ruled the Promised Land as an independent state before the arrival of the Romans. Members of this dynasty had built a palace for themselves in Jerusalem near the Temple.[26] Of course the days of Jewish independence were long

Hasmonean palace/Jerusalem palatial mansion excavation. It has been suggested that Herod Antipas stayed at the Hasmonean palace when he came to Jerusalem for Passover.

Hasmonean palace/Jerusalem palatial mansion excavations.

gone, but the Hasmonean palace had remained and likely had come into the possession of Herod the Great's family when he married the Jewish princess Mariamne.

We should in no way perceive that Pilate was extending some sort of political *favor* to Herod Antipas. Although that day the two men became friends, Luke points out that "before this they had been enemies" (Luke 23:12). Luke also provides reasons for the earlier animosity between these two Roman representatives. Certain Galileans who had come to offer sacrifices at the Temple in Jerusalem were killed at Pilate's direction, their blood mixing with the blood of their sacrifices (Luke 13:1). The Roman Jewish historian Philo mentions another incident that set these two men at odds with one another. In order to stir up trouble among the Jews of Jerusalem, Pilate had brought idolatrous gold shields into Jerusalem and installed them in his palace. The action was purportedly to honor the Roman emperor but in reality was intended to desecrate Jerusalem. Much to the chagrin of Pilate, Herod Antipas informed the Roman emperor, who subsequently ordered Pilate to remove the shields and return them to Caesarea Maritima.[27]

In this case, political expediency prevailed. Learning of Jesus's Galilean roots and knowing that the Galilean king, Antipas, was in Jerusalem, Pilate coaxed Antipas into taking the lead in this trial, thereby removing unwanted ramifications from himself. Pilate had received enough complaints about his rule that expedience dictated that Herod Antipas take the fall if an unpopular verdict against Jesus resulted in a riot. But Herod Antipas had troubles of his own. He had already executed one popular prophet of God—John the Baptist—and while he was interested in ridiculing and mocking Jesus, he was of no mind to take the lead in directing his death. Antipas's cruelty to Jesus, however, was right in line with Pilate's, whose desire was to eradicate all traces of Jewish observance.[28] Pilate and Antipas were both enemies of Jesus, so when Pilate sent Jesus to Antipas these one-time enemies became friends.

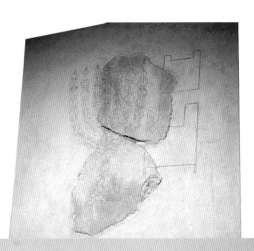

Menorah from the Hasmonean palace/Jerusalem palatial mansion, a possible location where Jesus was taken to see Herod Antipas.

© Dr. James C. Martin. The Wohl Archaeological Museum and Burnt House, Jerusalem.

◀ Excavation of first-century Tiberias. Herod Antipas traveled from Tiberias to Jerusalem for Passover.

PILATE MOCKS THE CHIEF PRIESTS AT THE JUDGE'S SEAT

MATTHEW 27:22–26

Pontius Pilate, the Roman governor, had something other than good hygiene in mind when he washed his hands at Jesus's trial. Most likely, this act performed at the judge's seat was meant to publicly mock those who were trying to manipulate him. In so doing, Pilate must have hoped to extract from them a political prize.

When Pilate took his official position at the judge's seat (Matt. 27:19), his action sent a commanding message.[29] This trial, or tribunal, had no jury; it was the Roman governor who entertained the charges, heard the evidence, and subsequently gave the verdict. Pilate could conduct the trial any way he saw fit, and he alone had the power to determine the outcome. The only law that governed Pilate's conduct was the Roman law against extortion.[30]

With this background in view, Matthew notes an unexpected strategy in the trial of Jesus. Instead of delivering a verdict, Pilate asked a question of the accusers: "What shall I do, then, with Jesus who is called

Mosaic from St. Peter in Gallicantu (Jerusalem), illustrating Pilate with Jesus at the judge's seat.

Christ?" (Matt. 27:22). The chief priests had been looking for ways to kill Jesus, but they were afraid a riot might ensue if they did it during Passover (Matt. 26:3–5). Pilate recognized their attempt to manipulate him and knew they would not hesitate to press their followers to demonstrate against him in order to force his weakened hand. Therefore, aware that the chief priests had delivered Jesus to him because of their envy (Mark 15:10), Pilate took water and washed his hands in front of them.

Pilate was not one to succumb to such pressure without achieving his own political goals,

Mosaic from St. Peter in Gallicantu (Jerusalem). After Caiaphas tore his clothes, the high priestly families took Jesus to Pilate for Roman involvement.

which is exactly why he washed his hands at the judge's seat, mimicking a ritual described in Deuteronomy 21:1–9. If a murder victim was found in the open country, the elders of the nearby villages were to measure the distance from the victim to the surrounding villages. The elders of the nearest village sacrificed a heifer and washed their hands over the heifer (v. 6) as they declared their innocence. "Our hands did not shed this blood, nor did our eyes see it done" (v. 7). According to the rite as later described in the Mishnah, the priests then confirmed their declaration of innocence.[31] In Pilate's parody, he washed his hands and declared, "I am innocent of this man's blood. . . . It is your responsibility!" At that point the crowd of the chief priests and their supporters shouted, "Let his blood be on us and on our children!" (Matt. 27:24–25).

Pilate's actions made it clear to the chief priests that he knew what they were up to. He might give them what they wanted, but first he would extract from them a political prize for himself. By the time the trade-off was over, Pilate ordered the crucifixion of Jesus, but he had what he wanted from the chief priests—total loyalty to Rome (John 19:15).

Statue of the emperor Tiberius. Although the chief priests had accused Jesus of blasphemy, it was they who rejected the living God and submitted to the direct imperial worship of Tiberius when they announced, "We have no king but Caesar."

Pilate may have used a Roman-style pan such as this one to wash his hands.

DELAYED VERDICT AT THE JUDGE'S SEAT

JOHN 18:29–19:16

Pilate was well aware that Jesus was a threat to Caiaphas and the other chief priests, and he was willing to entertain their request to kill Jesus. As the Roman procurator, however, Pilate was mindful of the importance of protecting his own hold on power. So Pilate set up his judge's seat at a place called the Stone Pavement on behalf of Rome, yet when he did so he delayed Caiaphas's request for a reason. A hasty and premature act could place Pilate in a weak position, so he used the proceedings to determine what could be gained from Caiaphas before acting on Caiaphas's demand.[32]

The precise location for the Stone Pavement is still somewhat uncertain, but more important than where it might have been located is what it represented. As an

Jerusalem model depicting the northern end of the Herodian palace, where Pilate set up his judge's seat.

© Dr. James C. Martin. Reproduction of the City of Jerusalem at the time of the Second Temple. (See full credit on page 4.)

imperial procurator, Pilate was a man of power whose judgment seat represented the power of Rome. When the accused stood before him, it was as if the defendant was standing before the emperor himself. Pilate's verdict could be overturned only by the Roman emperor, so when he informed Jesus that he had the power to release or convict him, Jesus knew that was true because of Pilate's authority within Rome's judicial system (John 19:10).

Yet Pilate was vulnerable because a long record of abuses of power had compromised this powerful man in this powerful place.[33] As a result, what he feared more than anything else was the prospect of Jewish citizens traveling to Rome and reporting the wide array of misconduct that attended his stay in office. Just such an embassy had been organized

Fourteenth-century marble depiction of the scourging of Jesus.

© Dr. James C. Martin. Musée du Louvre; Autorisation de photographer et de filmer—LOUVRE.

earlier. The Roman Jewish historian Philo summarizes what it meant to Pilate: "It was this final point which particularly exasperated him, for he feared that if they actually sent an embassy they would also expose the rest of his conduct as governor by stating in full the briberies, the insults, the robberies, the outrages and wanton injuries, the executions without trial constantly repeated, the ceaseless and supremely grievous cruelty."[34] Later, after the death and resurrection of Jesus, such a delegation was sent by the Samaritans to Rome in order to deal with Pilate's debauchery. As a result, Pilate was recalled to Rome.[35]

Now for Pilate, the judge's seat set on the Stone Pavement had only the appearance of power. He could ill afford to make a decision regarding Jesus that would cause him to lose his political position. Therefore, Pilate considered his options: instruct Caiaphas to kill Jesus (John 18:28–31); permit Herod Antipas to kill Jesus (Luke 23:6–12); or set Jesus free (Luke 23:13–22). When Pilate decided to let Jesus go, the crowd of chief priests and elders shouted, "If you let this man go, you are no friend of Caesar." In response to this threat Pilate asked, "Shall I crucify your king?" In error the chief priests had earlier charged the Son of God with blasphemy (Matt. 26:63–66). Now these same men committed blasphemy as they proclaimed, "We have no king but Caesar" (John 19:15).

With these words the high priests rejected the God of Abraham, Isaac, and Jacob and submitted to direct imperial cult by making the Roman emperor their god.[36] So there before the judgment seat of Rome on the Stone Pavement, Pilate heard the words that allowed him to kill Jesus and not worry about any political fallout.

Aerial view looking east of the towers located at the northern portion of Herod's palace, which later became Pontius Pilate's Jerusalem residence.

PART 8

THE CRUCIFIXION, RESURRECTION, AND ASCENSION OF JESUS

Tomb of Jesus in the Church of the Holy Sepulcher.

The days that surround the crucifixion, resurrection, and ascension of Jesus reshaped the world. While all four Gospels offer different highlights on the activities, character, and identity of Jesus, they each spend considerable time focused on the purpose for which he had come: "From that time on Jesus began to explain to his disciples that he must go to Jerusalem and . . . be killed and on the third day be raised to life" (Matt. 16:21). These inspired writers each pay special attention to events that happened where they did for a reason.

We begin part 8 with Jesus's crucifixion as we explore why he was crucified outside the city walls, in a cemetery, alongside a public roadway, and at a place called Golgotha. Clearly the place of his execution was not chosen haphazardly. Jesus was not the only one facing Roman charges, and so when he came to the place of execution, he was crucified between two criminals.

With a bold and powerful cry, Jesus gave up his spirit. When he did, a further set of events was set in motion. The large and heavy curtain in the Temple was torn in two. We will see why it was placed where it was and explore the significance of its rending. Jesus's death also motivated Joseph of Arimathea to seek custody of his body from the imperial Roman governor, Pontius Pilate, in order to bury him in Joseph's own tomb, and we will investigate why this happened. The chief priests and Pharisees who opposed Jesus had spent the week in conspiracies, maneuvering to have Jesus killed, but Jesus's death afforded them no rest as they sought to secure the tomb. We will investigate both the nature and rationale behind that security.

After the crucifixion, the third day dawned with startling news: Jesus was not in the tomb! He was risen, and for forty days following his resurrection he spoke with many people in many places. We will look at two of those instances, first inquiring into the purpose of his encounter with two men traveling on the road to Emmaus and then focusing our attention on Jesus as he met with the apostles at the Sea of Galilee.

After forty days of proving to them in many ways that he was actually alive, Jesus took one last walk with his disciples that culminated with his ascension. This group had often walked the road between Jerusalem and Bethany, but this time was different. When they reached the ridge of the Mount of Olives, Jesus blessed them and ascended into heaven, bringing his mission of rescue to completion.

No series of events in the history of the world has had a greater impact on our temporal and eternal destiny than these actions of Jesus, who through his crucifixion, resurrection, and ascension fulfilled God's long-standing promise to rescue the world from mutiny and death. We will see that each of these events in his sinless life happened where they did for a reason.

Ilustration of a *kokhim* tomb.

Rolling stone covering the entrance into a first-century tomb at Bethpage.

The Church of the Primacy of Peter commemorates Jesus's meeting with the disciples after his resurrection.

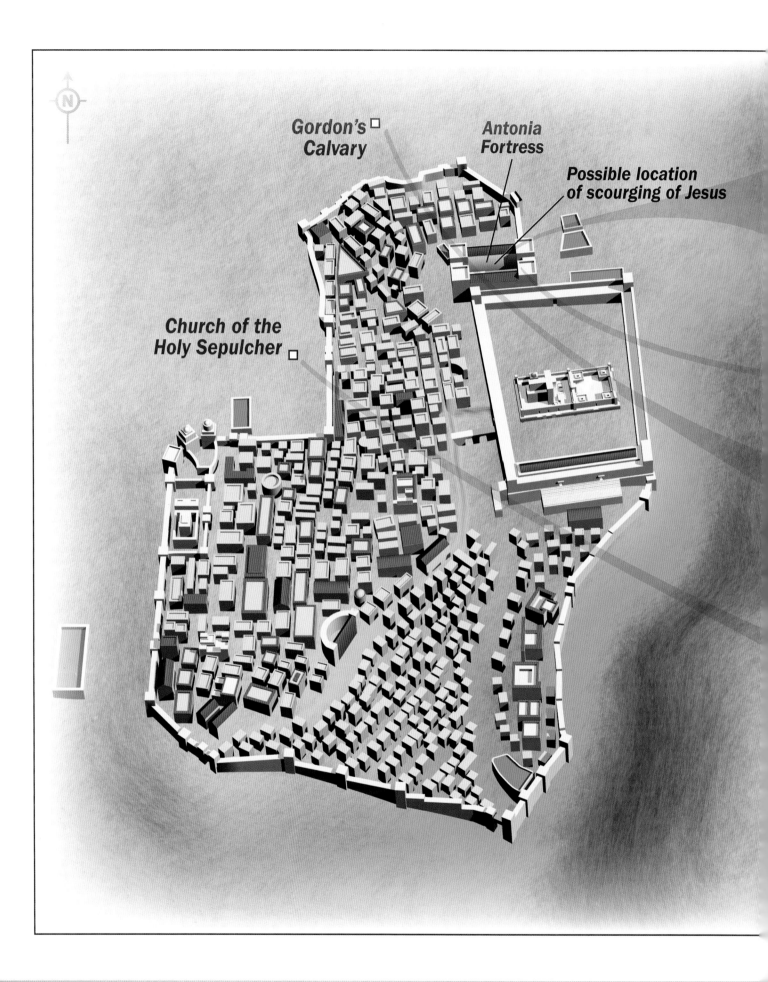

Gordon's Calvary

Antonia Fortress

Possible location of scourging of Jesus

Church of the Holy Sepulcher

Mosaic above the stone pavement of the Antonia Fortress (*Lithostrotos*), depicting Jesus taking up the cross.

Antonia Fortress model.

The Garden Tomb (Gordon's Calvary).

Entrance into the Church of the Holy Sepulcher.

CRUCIFIED AT GOLGOTHA

MATTHEW 27:33–44

As Jesus carried the cross to his place of execution, the Gospel writers spare us the most gruesome of the details. However, they do identify the location where Jesus was crucified. We will see that the Romans crucified Jesus at Golgotha for a reason.

The various names associated with the place of Jesus's execution all bring to mind the same picture. Jesus died at "The Place of the Skull" (Matt. 27:33). The Aramaic word is translated "Golgotha," and the Latin equivalent is "Calvary." Beyond that, we do not know if this reference to *skull* was meant to describe the shape of the hill or to identify this place as one regularly used

for public executions. What we do know is that from then on, Golgotha was best known for being the place where Jesus was crucified.

Two sites within Jerusalem have been associated with Jesus's death and resurrection: the Church of the Holy Sepulcher and Gordon's Calvary (the Garden Tomb). In the first century, believers in Jesus gathered on the site now covered by the Church of the Holy Sepulcher. In a bid to destroy the memories associated with the death and resurrection of Jesus, the emperor Hadrian renovated the site by shaving off the top of the hill and constructing a Roman temple and shrine on the

newly formed plateau. In 1883 General Charles Gordon pointed to a hill, associated with a garden and a tomb, that he believed was a more likely location for Calvary than the Church of the Holy Sepulcher.[1] Both these locations have things in common that help us understand why the Romans selected such a site for Jesus's crucifixion. At that time each was located outside the city walls of Jerusalem, linked to a cemetery, and along a public roadway.

First-century Jewish culture dictated that cemeteries be located outside the city walls[2] because contact with a dead body made one ritually unclean (Lev. 15:31; Num. 5:2; 9:6–7; 19:13). Based on this requirement, the cemetery at the base of the hill of Golgotha must have been located outside the city walls.[3] What better way to show Roman contempt of the Jews than to desecrate their cemeteries by crucifying Jews on their hallowed ground?

Another characteristic of Golgotha was its location along a public roadway—a fact that figured into the Roman selection of this site. For the Romans, crucifixion was a practice usually meant to serve as a deterrent to crime. Seneca asserts, "The more publicity punishments have, the more they avail as an admonition and a warning."[4] In the Jewish world, crucifixion was reprehensible not only because of the pain but also due to the shame brought on the victims, who were stripped of their clothes, hung on a cross, and publicly humiliated (see Deut. 21:23). The proximity to the public also provided the opportunity for Jesus's opponents to lash out at him, thereby fulfilling Psalm 22:6–8 (Matt. 27:39–43).

There were reasons the Romans carried out crucifixions at Golgotha. The Romans wanted to publicly humiliate their victims, and this cruel act was a warning to others of what lay ahead for those who challenged the power of Rome. Yet no matter what deterrents were attempted, Rome was not able to stop the outcome that forever changed the world at Golgotha.

This model of Golgotha reveals the rocky knoll located to the left of the roadway leading into ancient Jerusalem, where the Church of the Holy Sepulcher is located.

This model of Golgotha, associated with the Garden Tomb, is depicted as the rocky hill near the center of the photo.

◀ Aerial view looking north toward the entrance to the Church of the Holy Sepulcher, which was built over one of the suggested sites of Jesus's tomb.

CRUCIFIED BETWEEN TWO CRIMINALS

LUKE 23:32–43

Given the weighty importance of Jesus's crucifixion, we might well expect to find a lone cross occupying Golgotha. But God had a different plan. Jesus was not crucified alone but between two criminals for a reason.

Luke invites us to follow Jesus through the time of his arrest, trials, and execution. At first it might appear that Jesus was the only one enmeshed in Roman legal proceedings that day. But when we arrive at Golgotha, Luke expands our view and we see that two others had faced Roman charges and capital punishment that same day. "Two other men, both criminals, were also led out with him to be executed. When they came to the place called the Skull, there they crucified him, along with the criminals—one on his right, the other on his left" (Luke 23:32–33).

In the midst of what had become an avalanche of deceit, hateful words, and images of despair as Jesus hung on the cross, one of the criminals advocated the truth of Jesus's identity and asked Jesus to remember him in God's Kingdom (Luke 23:42). Every step in the Roman judicial process was meant to demean Jesus and undermine his credibility. They beat him,

mocked him, placed a crown of thorns on his head, stripped him of his clothes, and put a sign above his head denoting the crime of which he was accused. One of the criminals added to this barrage of criticism by attacking Jesus's identity even as they hung dying. A real Messiah whom people could count on, he cursed, would be able to save himself and those condemned beside him (Luke 23:39). It was the second criminal, on Jesus's other side, who voiced the message that they were killing the Son of God. In rebuking the criminal who had scorned Jesus, this man said, "We are punished justly, for we are getting what our deeds deserve. But this man has done nothing wrong" (Luke 23:41). Jesus may have been treated like a criminal, but even with all appearances to the contrary, he had done nothing wrong.

The presence of the two criminals with Jesus at Golgotha also affirmed his teaching about acceptance and rejection in God's Kingdom[5] and acted as a reminder of the many illustrations and parables in which Jesus had spoken of those who would be brought into the

The painting *Crucifixion* (1552–53) by Leonard Limousin, showing Jesus between two criminals.

© Dr. James C. Martin. Musée du Louvre; Autorisation de photographer et de filmer—LOUVRE.

Kingdom and those who would not. He had earlier taught about the sheep being separated to his right and the goats to his left (Matt. 25:31–46), just as tares would be separated from the wheat (Matt. 13:30) and bad fish from good (Matt. 13:48). Even at this culminating moment, the sight of Jesus crucified between two men with one accepting Jesus as the Messiah and one rejecting him reminds us of the truth of his teaching.[6] So it was that Jesus died between two criminals for a reason.

Sardines. After the catch, the good (i.e., kosher) fish were to be separated from the bad (i.e., nonkosher) fish.

Sheep grazing along with goats. At the end of the day, shepherds separate the sheep from the goats before entering the sheepfold.

This grain field contains both the wheat and the tares.

JESUS DIES ON A CROSS

MARK 15:24

he earliest record we have of crucifixion in Israel comes not at the hands of the Romans but of a Jewish king—Alexander Jannaeus, who ruled from 103 BC to 76 BC.[7] However, it is within Roman literature that we find the most frequent mention of crucifixion as governors, generals, and emperors used it to punish and manipulate those they sought to control.[8]

Crucifixion was a well-known form of punishment throughout the Roman world. Weakened through blood loss and de-fleshing caused by the repeated beatings with a Roman scourge or *flagellum*, the accused was led to a structure on which the crossbeam was raised into place. In Jesus's case, the soldiers used nails to secure him to the wood.[9] We know a bit more about what this may have meant for Jesus due to a 1968 excavation that unearthed the remains of a first-century Jewish man who had been crucified. A nail had been driven through this man's heel bone into the vertical portion of an olive-tree cross, with a small piece of wood used as a washer

between the head of the nail and the ankle. The pain and suffering associated with this kind of death are unimaginable.[10]

Certainly the physical pain of crucifixion served as a deterrent in and of itself, but this form of execution also carried with it a stigma that clouded the death of the accused. In the laws recorded in Deuteronomy, God made it clear that anyone who was executed by being hung on a tree was to be regarded as under God's curse (Deut. 21:22–23). Paul connects Jesus's death to this Scripture: "Christ redeemed us from the curse of the law by becoming a curse for us, for it is written: 'Cursed is everyone who is hung on a tree'" (Gal. 3:13). As the Jewish believers in Jesus carried that message to those living beyond the boundaries of the Promised Land, they had to deal with the incongruity of pointing people to a crucified Savior. Paul asserts that he is not ashamed of the gospel of salvation through Jesus Christ (Rom. 1:16). Although this message of the cross is "foolishness to those who are perishing, . . . it is the power of God" to those being rescued from the works of the adversary (1 Cor. 1:18; see also 1 John 3:8).

So why did Jesus die on a cross when this form of death destined

Crucifixion on an olive tree. The Jewish ruler Alexander Jannaeus crucified Pharisees on olive trees lining the road from Jerusalem to Bethlehem.

© Dr. James C. Martin. Illustration by Timothy Ladwig.

According to tradition, Peter was crucified upside down on an X-shaped cross.

© Dr. James C. Martin. Illustration by Timothy Ladwig.

him to so much pain and shame? Perhaps we need to look no farther than Isaiah 53 and John 3 for an explanation. Isaiah establishes what to expect of the coming Messiah: "He had no beauty or majesty to attract us to him, nothing in his appearance that we should desire him. He was despised and rejected by men, a man of sorrows, and familiar with suffering. Like one from whom men hide their faces he was despised, and we esteemed him not" (Isa. 53:2–3). In his death, Jesus did not dodge such pain and shame. He had earlier explained to Nicodemus about himself: "Just as Moses lifted up the snake in the desert, so the Son of Man must be lifted up, that everyone who believes in him may have eternal life" (John 3:14–15).

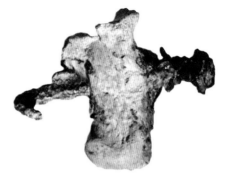

First-century skeletal remains of a heel bone, which contains the nail and the remnant of a wooden plank used to secure the foot to a cross.

Skeletal model depicting how the nail went through the wooden plank and heel bone in the process of crucifixion.

Fourteenth-century carving of the crucifixion of Christ on a T-shaped cross.

TEARING THE TEMPLE CURTAIN

MATTHEW 27:45–51

As Jesus hung on the cross, for three hours a thick, unnatural darkness blanketed the land, and when he died the earth shook so violently that rocks split apart (Matt. 27:45, 51). We might well expect that God's Temple would also respond in some way to the horrible events of this day. "And when Jesus had cried out again in a loud voice, he gave up his spirit. At that moment the curtain of the temple was torn in two from top to bottom" (Matt. 27:50–51). The Temple curtain was torn in two for a reason.

This curtain formed a fabric wall that separated the two rooms in the Temple proper: the Holy Place and the Holy of Holies. God had given Moses special instructions regarding the construction and design of that curtain. A skilled weaver was to produce this curtain as one piece using blue, purple, and scarlet yarn together with finely twisted linen (Exod. 26:31). Later Jewish writings further describe the appearance of this Temple curtain during the time of the Gospels. The Mishnah portrays the curtain as a wall consisting of two fabric

Model of the Jerusalem Temple, with the Gate Beautiful in the foreground, Nicanor Gate in the center, and the gate entrance into the sanctuary in the background.

layers, one in front of the other, separated by a distance of approximately eighteen inches.[11] This curtain wall was massive in scale—sixty feet long and thirty feet wide—and highly durable, with each layer composed of seventy-two joined squares.[12]

The architecture and design of the Temple taught people about God's character and nature. The inner room of the Temple was the place that particularly represented his holiness.

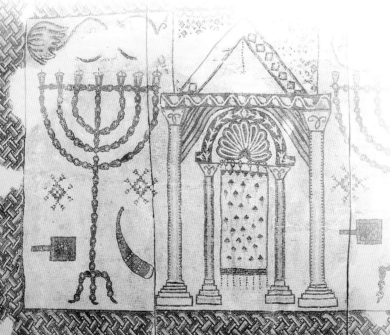

Second- or third-century mosaic of the Temple curtain dividing the sanctuary from the Holy of Holies.

© Dr. James C. Martin. Collection of the Israel Museum, Jerusalem, and courtesy of the Israel Antiquities Authority, exhibited at the Israel Museum, Jerusalem.

© Dr. James C. Martin. Reproduction of the City of Jerusalem at the time of the Second Temple. (See full credit on page 4.)

Because God is holy and his people were not, this room had the most restricted access of any place in the Temple complex. Only the high priest was allowed to enter, and even his access was limited to the solemn Day of Atonement, the one day per year when he carried blood into this room to atone for humanity's mutiny against God (see Genesis 3; Lev. 16:15–17; Heb. 9:7–8).

So why did this curtain tear from top to bottom when Jesus died? This description is significant because a Jewish father would tear his clothing from top to bottom when he received the horrible news of his son's death.[13] While necessary for the rescue of the world, the crucifixion and death of Jesus caused his Father untold pain. Therefore, the tearing of the Temple curtain may represent an expression of the heavenly Father's grief at the death of his Son.[14]

This tearing of the curtain also provides a physical and visual sign that the purpose of the Messiah Jesus had been fulfilled. The writer of the book of Hebrews records that the tearing of this curtain was the sign that all those who belong to Jesus can now confidently enter God's presence. "We have confidence to enter the Most Holy Place by the blood of Jesus, by a new and living way opened for us through the curtain, that is, his body" (Heb. 10:19–20).

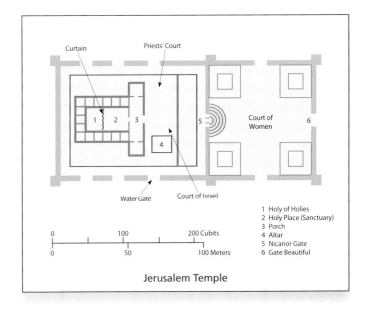

Jerusalem Temple

1 Holy of Holies
2 Holy Place (Sanctuary)
3 Porch
4 Altar
5 Nicanor Gate
6 Gate Beautiful

The tearing of the Temple curtain had a purpose. Its rending reminds us of the mourning of a Father over his Son. Moreover, it was a sign that the heavenly Father's promise of redemption and restoration of humanity had been completed through the Messiah Jesus (John 1:35–41), whom God sent to open the door for us to directly enter into his presence.

Model of the Ark of the Covenant. The original ark (box) was located behind the Temple curtain.

JOSEPH OF ARIMATHEA GOES TO PILATE

JOHN 19:38–41

Within Jewish culture of the first century, the task of preparing a body for burial fell to the grief-laden hands of family and friends. So when word spread that Jesus had been killed, Joseph of Arimathea claimed the body, prepared it for burial, and placed Jesus's remains in his own unoccupied tomb. We will see that he did so for a reason.

The Gospel writers provide significant details surrounding Joseph of Arimathea's involvement in the burial of Jesus. Although a prominent member of the Sanhedrin council, Joseph of Arimathea did not concur in seeking the death of Jesus (Luke 23:50–51; see also Mark 15:43). Neither priest nor rabbi, he was a rich land owner who was a disciple of Jesus. Up until the time of Jesus's arrest, Joseph had kept that relationship a secret due to his fear of the chief priests in opposition to Jesus (John 19:38). Wealthy men such as Joseph of Arimathea had direct access to Roman officials. Now with boldness he proceeded to Pilate, from whom he requested and received the body of Jesus for burial.

It was already late in the afternoon, and the start of Sabbath was

Evidence of *kokhim* tombs inside the Church of the Holy Sepulcher.

Fourteenth-century marble carving depicting Joseph of Arimathea taking Jesus from the cross.

about to begin. Because he had a newly hewn tomb in the cemetery where Jesus had been executed and because a body could not be left on a cross when Passover commenced, Joseph had to act quickly (Deut. 21:23; Luke 23:56). Evidence of *kokhim* tombs dating from 40 BC to AD 41 is found within the Church of the Holy Sepulcher—one of the possible locations of Jesus's crucifixion, burial, and resurrection.[15] A *kokhim* tomb consisted of a chamber with a low bench carved around the inside walls that provided a surface on which the body might be placed for preparation. Once preparations were completed, the deceased was slid into one of the narrow horizontal shafts deep enough to hold the body. The body remained there for a year or more while the softer tissue decomposed. The family then returned to the tomb and placed the bones into an ossuary, which was a small limestone box that became the permanent resting place for the remains.[16] Joseph brought Jesus to just such a tomb where his body was put on the preparation bench, treated with a mixture of myrrh and aloes, and then wrapped in linen (John 19:39–40).[17]

Unlike the disciples, who had publicly followed Jesus, Joseph of Arimathea had followed Jesus secretly.

Relief of the body of Christ and the preparation of his grave.

© Dr. James C. Martin. Musée du Louvre; Autorisation de photographer et de filmer—LOUVRE.

Yet after the crucifixion, here he was, stepping forward in devotion to the Messiah, the sent one (John 8:42; 12:44; 17:3, 21, 25). "Joseph of Arimathea, a prominent member of the Council, who was himself waiting for the Kingdom of God, went boldly to Pilate and asked for Jesus' body" (Mark 15:43). This action made it clear to the chief priests that Joseph's loyalty to Jesus superseded his loyalty to them. At just the time Jesus's disciples scattered in fear, Joseph of Arimathea thrust aside his fear and openly requested the body of Jesus from the very man who had ordered Jesus's execution.

Ivory statuette (ca. AD 1260) of Nicodemus, who helped Joseph of Arimathea with the body of Jesus.

Excavated remains on the Mount of Olives of a *kokhim* tomb and bone boxes known as ossuaries.

SECURITY AT THE TOMB

MATTHEW 27:62–66

The chief priests and certain others of the Temple leadership had carefully planned a strategy to rid themselves of Jesus. Given the incredible popularity of Jesus, his opponents had to plan his arrest so as to avoid an open riot from his multitude of followers (Matt. 26:3–5). Once Jesus was arrested, these religious leaders decided to manipulate the situation so that the Roman governor, Pilate, would carry out the death sentence of Jesus. But even when Pilate did just that, the opponents of Jesus were still not rid of the threat Jesus presented. They demanded security for the tomb.

This security established by Jesus's opponents had three physical components. The first was a blocking stone—a heavy stone that may have been a square stone that turned on a hinge or a round stone that rolled in a track. In either case, the stone was large enough and heavy enough to discourage entry into the tomb (Mark 16:3–4).[18] The second layer of security was the seal prohibiting unauthorized persons from entering the tomb. And the final element of security involved sentries. Because certain members from the chief priests and Pharisees had gone to Pilate with a request to place a guard at the tomb, it has often been assumed that this guard was composed of Roman soldiers. But Pilate's response was more ambiguous regarding the composition of the guard. He may well have directed the chief priests to place their own Jewish Temple guard at the tomb (Matt. 27:65).[19]

The reason the Temple leadership asked to have the tomb of Jesus secured certainly had something to do with the general protection offered tombs by the Roman government. A twenty-four-by-fifteen-inch marble tablet first became known near Nazareth in 1878 and is referred to as the "Nazareth Inscription."[20] There is strong evidence that it dates to the first century AD, and the tablet states the Roman legal point of view on this topic: no unauthorized person was to enter or disturb any tomb. "If, however, anyone charges that another has

Monumental tomb of the priestly family of Jason.

either demolished them [tombs], or has in any other way extracted the buried, or has maliciously transferred them to other places in order to wrong them, or has displaced the sealing of other stones. . . . In the case of violation I desire that the offender be sentenced to capital punishment on charge of violation of the sepulture [burial]."[21]

These layers of security were to function together to achieve one purpose. The opponents of Jesus knew that he had promised to rise on the third day, so they told Pilate they were worried the disciples would steal the body and claim he had been raised from the dead (Matt. 27:63–64). Because Joseph of Arimathea—a follower of

Jesus and a powerful, wealthy, and influential member of the Council—had control of Jesus's body, the chief priests suspected an imminent plot to steal the body. The oppositional stance of the chief priests was so great that when they heard the witness of their soldiers, they bribed them to lie about what they had seen (Matt. 28:4, 12–15). But no security system of humankind could thwart God's plan (Matt. 28:6, 11). Paradoxically, it was the security measures initiated by these enemies of Jesus that established the validity of his resurrection. The testimonies of the Temple guards provided a message that could not be held back but was propelled around the world.

Rolling-stone door used to cover a tomb.

Marble representation (AD 1572) of the resurrection of Christ.

FROM JERUSALEM
TO EMMAUS AND BACK

MARK 16:9–14; LUKE 24:13–48

Two followers of Jesus had heard some of the women report what had occurred at the tomb that morning: Jesus's body was missing, and angels had said he was alive (Luke 24:23–24)! These two men had left the group and headed for the village of Emmaus.

Walking the seven miles from Jerusalem to Emmaus (Luke 24:13) provided the men time for reviewing the events of the past week. As they walked, a third man joined them whom they did not recognize. They were amazed he did not know what had just occurred in Jerusalem. But their new companion, who seemed so in the dark, proved to be the one who provided illumination (John 12:46). The two men had all the facts but lacked a context that would give those facts meaning. The unrecognized Jesus asked them, "Did not the Christ have to suffer these things and then enter his glory?" (Luke 24:26). So starting with Moses and all the prophets, he taught them about himself (Luke 24:27).

As the three travelers approached the village of Emmaus,[22] Jesus seemed to continue on his way. But since it was almost evening, the other two encouraged him to stay with them in the village. After entering the house, they gathered at the table where Jesus "took bread, gave thanks, broke it and began to give it to them" (Luke 24:30). As he broke the bread the two men recognized Jesus, whereupon he disappeared from their sight. In their excitement the two men hurried back to Jerusalem and spoke with the remaining apostles (referred to as the Eleven) and the others among them (Luke 24:33). While they were speaking, Jesus stood among them and said, "Peace be with you" (Luke 24:36).

It is significant that Jesus did not first show himself to the apostles. These men had been at the Master's feet as he taught. They had walked the country with him and personally witnessed his many miracles, and meal after meal they had fellowshipped with him. Yet on the morning Jesus rose from the dead, it was the women who first saw him and who were sent from his tomb with a message (Luke 23:55; 24:1, 10).

Mary Magdalene and another Mary had met the resurrected

Twelfth-century marble capital of the angel meeting the women at the tomb.

Roman road near the village of Emmaus (Qubeibeh).

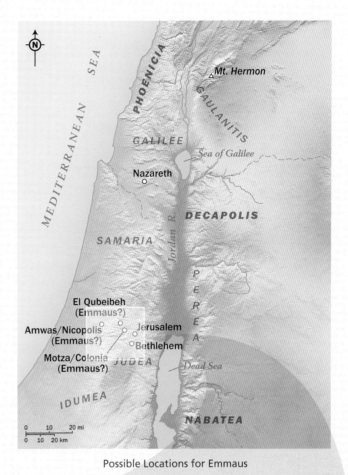

Possible Locations for Emmaus

Messiah and worshiped him (Matt. 28:1, 9). They were instructed to tell the disciples that Jesus was risen and to go to Galilee, where he would meet them. Then Jesus walked with the two men on the road to Emmaus. When Jesus opened their eyes, they immediately went back to Jerusalem and told the Eleven and those with them that Jesus had risen. Jesus then joined them in Jerusalem and continued to open their hearts to all the Scriptures said of him (Luke 24:44–47).

The Eleven learned a valuable lesson as the message of the resurrection went from Jerusalem to Emmaus and back—that others could be faithful witnesses even when the truth seemed impossible to believe and the messenger appeared unbelievable (Mark 16:14). They experienced firsthand that the Lord would use everyone who was willing to proclaim the proofs of Jesus's resurrection and power and that his messengers would never be limited to a small, select group.

JESUS MEETS THE APOSTLES IN THE GALILEE

JOHN 21

When we look carefully, we find an important detail tucked in among the things Jesus said the night he was arrested: "After I have risen, I will go ahead of you into Galilee" (Matt. 26:32; Mark 14:28). That detail shows up again on the day of Jesus's resurrection. The angel told the women who had come to the tomb to remind the disciples that they were to meet Jesus in the Galilee (Matt. 28:7; Mark 16:7). Jesus himself appeared to the women shortly after that and said, "Go and tell my brothers to go to Galilee; there they will see me" (Matt. 28:10). Clearly this was a matter of some importance. Though Jesus had already shown the disciples his resurrected body and had continued to teach them in Jerusalem (Mark 16:14; Luke 24:33–47), he wanted to meet the apostles in the Galilee for a reason.

The remaining days of the disciples' lives were defined by the meeting in the Galilee. It had been their great privilege to personally listen to Jesus, observe his actions, and ask him questions. They were his emissaries who were responsible for sharing his message with others—something with which they already had some limited

The modern Church of the Primacy of Peter, built on the bedrock foundation of earlier remains of the fourth- and seventh-century churches.

experience. Jesus had sent them to witness among their fellow Israelites announcing that the Kingdom of heaven was near, but he gave specific instructions to avoid the Gentiles or any town of the Samaritans (Matt. 10:5–7). This restriction no longer held (Matt. 10:18–20). God had declared that all peoples on earth would be blessed through his promise to Abraham (Gen. 12:3; John 8:56; Rom. 1:16; Gal. 3:14). The disciples, who had enjoyed the honor of walking and talking with Jesus, now had the privilege as sons of Abraham of walking among the Gentiles and talking about Jesus. The commission was clearly set in these memorable words, "Go and make disciples of all nations" (Matt. 28:19).

This calling to a broader outreach occurred in the same place where they had received their initial call to follow Jesus and be his disciples. In fact, a comparison

Early-twentieth-century fishing boat on the Sea of Galilee, similar to the type of boat the disciples used when Jesus met them in Galilee after his resurrection.

Aerial view (looking north) of the Church of the Primacy of Peter (red-roofed building in center). The north shore of the Sea of Galilee in this photo is known as Heptapegon, the traditional location where Jesus met the apostles after his resurrection.

of Luke 5:1–11 and John 21:3–6 shows striking parallels. In both cases a number of these men had been out fishing on the Sea of Galilee. Although they had caught nothing after fishing all night, they listened to the voice of Jesus and tried one more time. When they did, the net was so full of fish that it was ready to burst. In the first instance, Jesus called his disciples to fish for people (Matt. 4:19; Mark 1:17; Luke 5:10). With the same setting along the Sea of Galilee,[23] Jesus used a parallel experience to call these men again to fish for people.

The location highlights the audience to whom the apostles were to take the news about Jesus. The district west of the Sea of Galilee was known as "the Galilee of the Gentiles." This was a specific name for a region that had received this title due to the frequency with which it absorbed the conquest and occupation of Gentile invaders (Isa. 9:1–2; Matt. 4:15–16).[24] Thus this location underscores the reason why Jesus sent his disciples back to the

Galilee. He used this location to recall them to service and to remind them that their purpose was to carry the news of rescue even to the Gentiles.

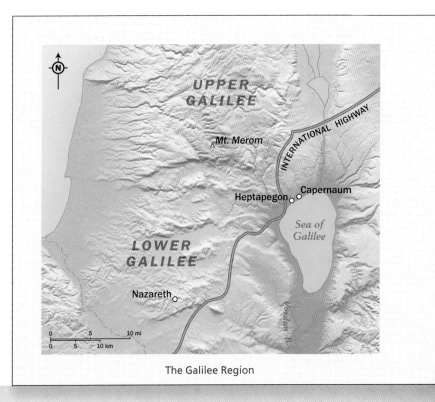

The Galilee Region

JESUS ASCENDS FROM THE MOUNT OF OLIVES

LUKE 24:50–51; ACTS 1:1–12

During the forty days following his resurrection, Jesus met both individuals and groups of people in order to assure his beloved followers with convincing proof that he was alive, as well as to give them instructions through the Holy Spirit (Matt. 28:9; Luke 24:15, 33–36; Acts 1:1–3). If these postresurrection visits had simply stopped, the disciples would have lacked the necessary closure to move on with the next steps in their lives. So there was one final time together before Jesus left them to return to his Father's house. His physical presence with the disciples ended with his ascension—an event that took place from the Mount of Olives for a reason.

View of Jerusalem looking west from above the Mount of Olives.

Jesus knew this time of transition would be difficult for his disciples, so he had prepared them for this moment. Just days earlier he had spoken to them about going away to prepare a place for them and then returning to bring them to that place (John 14:2–3). Furthermore, he noted that his departure was necessary so that the Counselor, the Spirit of Truth, could come to bring them power, to help them recall all the things they had seen and heard, and to bring clarity to his teaching (John 14:16–17, 25–26; Acts 1:8).

Forty days after the resurrection, Jesus led the disciples out of Jerusalem to a place on the familiar road toward Bethany. He raised his hands and blessed them, and then before their eyes, he ascended from the surface of the earth and was

hidden from their sight by a cloud (Luke 24:50–51; Acts 1:9).

The ridge of the Mount of Olives above Jerusalem is the likely location of this event. From the fourth century to the present, a series of churches has commemorated the location of Jesus's ascension.[25] Given the biblical evidence that places this event between Bethany and Jerusalem (Luke 24:50; Acts 1:12), these early church sites seem to take us to the right place.

Since we so often find an important connection between events in Jesus's life and their settings, it seems appropriate that we look for meaningfulness in the location of his ascension as well. First

Depiction (AD 1424) of the ascension of Jesus and final judgment.

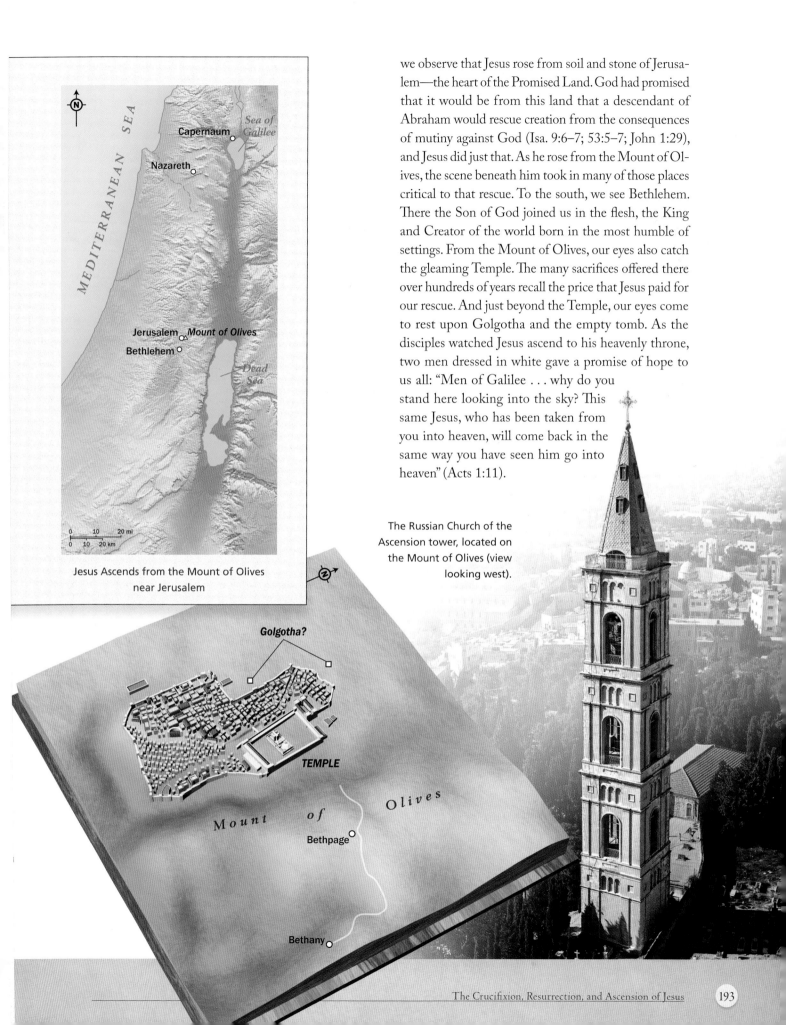

Jesus Ascends from the Mount of Olives
near Jerusalem

we observe that Jesus rose from soil and stone of Jerusalem—the heart of the Promised Land. God had promised that it would be from this land that a descendant of Abraham would rescue creation from the consequences of mutiny against God (Isa. 9:6–7; 53:5–7; John 1:29), and Jesus did just that. As he rose from the Mount of Olives, the scene beneath him took in many of those places critical to that rescue. To the south, we see Bethlehem. There the Son of God joined us in the flesh, the King and Creator of the world born in the most humble of settings. From the Mount of Olives, our eyes also catch the gleaming Temple. The many sacrifices offered there over hundreds of years recall the price that Jesus paid for our rescue. And just beyond the Temple, our eyes come to rest upon Golgotha and the empty tomb. As the disciples watched Jesus ascend to his heavenly throne, two men dressed in white gave a promise of hope to us all: "Men of Galilee . . . why do you stand here looking into the sky? This same Jesus, who has been taken from you into heaven, will come back in the same way you have seen him go into heaven" (Acts 1:11).

The Russian Church of the Ascension tower, located on the Mount of Olives (view looking west).

Golgotha?

TEMPLE

Mount of Olives

Bethpage

Bethany

NOTES

Part 1 The Birth and Early Years of Jesus

1. A full discussion of the narrative flow of the Bible and additional primary sources used throughout this manuscript can be found in James C. Martin, *Exploring Bible Times: The Gospels in Context.* For further information, please email bibleworldseminars@gmail.com.

2. Examples include Genesis 5, 10; 1 Chronicles, Ezra, and Nehemiah.

3. For a further discussion of the relationship between genealogy and Israelite culture, see James C. Martin, *Exploring Bible Times*, 44–46.

4. Josephus, *The Life of Flavius Josephus* 1:6.

5. Joachim Jeremias, *Jerusalem in the Time of Jesus* (Philadelphia: Fortress Press, 1969), 214. See also Josephus, *Against Apion* 1:7.

6. Josephus, *Against Apion* 1:31. The prospective wife's line had to be traced through a total of eight mothers: "Her mother, mother's mother, mother's father's mother, and this one's [the priest's] mother; also her father's mother and this one's [the priest's] mother." Mishnah, *Kiddushin* 4:4.

7. "The priestly, Levitic, and Israelitish stocks may intermarry; the proselyte, freedman, . . . may all intermarry." Mishnah, *Kiddushin* 4:1.

8. Josephus, *Life* 1:6.

9. Mishnah, *Yebamoth* 4:13.

10. Mishnah, *Tanith* 4:5; usually during the month of July.

11. Eusebius, *The History of the Church from Christ to Constantine*, 1.7.13.

12. When King Uzziah's pride got in the way of his obedience to God, he entered the Temple to burn incense on this altar and became a leper as a result (2 Chron. 26:16–20).

13. Mishnah, *Tamid* 5:2.

14. For an in-depth discussion of these activities, see Jeremias, *Jerusalem in the Time of Jesus*, 201n, 206.

15. Alfred Edersheim, *The Life and Times of Jesus the Messiah* (Grand Rapids: Eerdmans, 1971), 1:134.

16. Bargil Pixner, *With Jesus Through Galilee According to the Fifth Gospel* (Rosh Pina, Israel: Corazin Publishing, 1992), 14–15.

17. For a summary of Herod's era, see Ben Witherington III, *New Testament History: A Narrative Account* (Grand Rapids: Baker Academic, 2001), 53–61.

18. Macrobius, *Saturnalia*, 2.4.11. Herod, claiming Jewish ancestry, held regard for the prohibition against pork but apparently had no such prohibitions against killing his sons!

19. Gideon Foerster, "Herodium," in *The New Encyclopedia of Archaeological Excavations in the Holy Land*, ed. E. Stern (Jerusalem: Carta, 1993), 618.

20. Edersheim, *Life and Times of Jesus the Messiah*, 1:85.

21. Martin, *Exploring Bible Times*, 51.

22. The betrothal was usually to an extended family member (Josephus, *Against Apion* 2:200), and the contract was done by one's own act or through an agent (Mishnah, *Kiddushin* 2:1). The girl was to remain out of public view (Philo, *De Specialibus III*, 169) and have no physical or relational contact with any person of the opposite gender (Mishnah, *Ketubot* 7:6).

23. Mishnah, *Ketubot* 5:2; Mishnah, *Kiddushin* 2:1; Babylonian Talmud, *Pesahim* 113a; Mishnah, *Aboth* 5:21.

24. "These are they that are to be stoned . . . he that has a connection with a girl that is betrothed." Mishnah, *Sanhedrin* 7:4a.

25. The social stigma of the circumstances of his birth followed Jesus into his adult life (John 8:41). But the current threat of execution was very real for Mary. If Joseph did not divorce her, he would be considered the father, thus putting the two of them at risk for execution. Since Joseph went ahead and took Mary as his wife, rabbinic literature states that Joseph and Mary had committed adultery: "She, who was a descendant of princes and governors, played the harlot with carpenters." Babylonian Talmud, *Sanhedrin* 106a.

26. Hannah lived in the hill country of Ephraim, while Elizabeth lived in the hill country of Judea. There is a geographical connection between the home of Hannah in Ramathaim (Ramah) and the traditional home of Elizabeth at Ein Kerem. On Ein Kerem, see Jack Finegan, *The Archeology of the New Testament: The Life of Jesus and the Beginning of the Early Church*, 2nd ed. (Princeton, NJ: Princeton University Press, 1992), 3–4.

27. Martin, *Exploring Bible Times*, 65.

28. Writing about AD 150, Justin Martyr seems to have taken this position. See *Dialogue with Trypho* 78.

29. Grottoes serve to screen against uncleanness. Mishnah, *Oholoth* 8:1–6.

30. Early Christian writers from the second through the fifth century such as Justin Martyr, Origen, and Jerome all provide witness of a specific cave in Bethlehem associated with Jesus's birth. For a discussion of their contribution, see John McRay, *Archaeology and the New Testament* (Grand Rapids: Baker, 1991), 156.

The cave in which Jesus was born may very well lie beneath the Church of the Nativity in Bethlehem. Emperor Hadrian (AD 135) attempted to eliminate the memory of Jesus's birth at this location by building a pagan worship site there dedicated to Adonis (Venus). But his efforts to eliminate the memory only served to mark the birth cave of Jesus, waiting for the day of Emperor Constantine when a Byzantine church was built there (AD 339). A Christian church has continuously marked this cave from the fourth century to the present. Jerome Murphy-O'Connor, *The Holy Land: An Oxford Archaeological Guide from the Earliest Times to 1700*, 4th ed. (Oxford: Oxford University Press, 1998), 200–201.

31. The information in this chapter is adapted from Martin, *Exploring Bible Times*, 63–64.

32. Victor H. Matthews and Don C. Benjamin, *Social World of Ancient Israel 1250–587 BCE* (Peabody, MA: Hendrickson, 1993), 55.

33. The traditional location of the Shepherds Field has been marked by a number of early Christian worship sites. For more information, see Finegan, *Archeology of the New Testament*, 42–43.

34. Edersheim, *Life and Times of Jesus the Messiah*, 1:186.

35. "If cattle [sheep and goats] are found between Jerusalem and as far as Migdal Eder [Bethlehem], or within the like distance in any direction, males must be deemed to be Whole-offerings and females Peace-offerings. R. Judah says: If fitted to be Passover-offerings, they must be deemed to be Passover-offerings [if they are found during] thirty days before the feast." Mishnah, *Shekalim* 7:4.

36. "Abba Gorion of Zaidan says in the name of Abba Guria: A man should not teach his son to be an ass-driver or a camel-driver, or a barber or a sailor, or a herdsman or a shopkeeper, for their craft is the craft of robbers." Mishnah, *Kiddushin* 4:14. "None may buy wool or milk from herdsmen." Mishnah, *Baba Kamma* 10:9.

37. Jeremias, *Jerusalem in the Time of Jesus*, 164.

38. Alfred Edersheim, *The Temple: Its Ministry and Services as They Were at the Time of Jesus Christ* (Grand Rapids: Eerdmans, 1978), 345.

39. This chapter is adapted from Martin, *Exploring Bible Times*, 72–74. The identification of these men as Persian is supported by second-century Christian art found in the catacombs of Rome that depict these visitors in Persian garments. The reason the invading Persians spared the Church of the Nativity in Bethlehem (AD 614) was that they saw a mosaic depicting the Magi who were wearing Persian headdress. Paul L. Maier, *In the Fullness of Time: A Historian Looks at Christmas, Easter, and the Early Church* (San Francisco: HarperCollins, 1991), 48.

40. Some suggest the Magi were looking at the collocation of Jupiter, Saturn, and Mars in the constellation Pisces that occurred in 6 BC. Jupiter was associated with kingship and Pisces with Palestine. Maier, *In the Fullness of Time*, 54–55.

41. Neither Joseph nor Mary saw Jesus during the first day of travel, and it then took a full day for them to return to Jerusalem. "After three days they found him in the temple courts" (Luke 2:46).

42. This gave the family time to worship together and to reflect on the great things God had done for Israel (Deut. 16:1–8).

43. Jeremias, *Jerusalem in the Time of Jesus*, 76. See also Mishnah, *Yoma* 8:4; *Niddah* 5:6.

44. The Temple built by Solomon was destroyed by the Babylonians in 586 BC. It was rebuilt and rededicated seventy years later in 516 BC.

45. Jeremias, *Jerusalem in the Time of Jesus*, 81.

Part 2 Jesus Reveals His Legitimate Authority

1. John the Baptist was born of priestly lineage—his father, Zechariah, was from the priestly house of Abijah and his mother, Elizabeth, was from the priestly house of Aaron (Luke 1:5).

2. 2 Macc. 4:7–17.

3. See also 2 Kings 1:7–8; Matt. 3:4; Josephus, *Jewish War* (hereafter *J. W.*) 5:231, 232, 235. For a discussion of John's distinctive diet, see Martin, *Exploring Bible Times*, 83–84.

4. *Miqvaot* 1:6, 8.

5. *Miqvaot* 5:5. The water could not be drawn by hand from a pool. McRay, *Archaeology and the New Testament*, 49.

6. In first-century Judaism, people underwent ritual washing in order to identify with the doctrinal position of a teacher or to show one's submission to the authority of a particular rabbi. Furthermore, Gentiles who wished to convert to Judaism underwent proselyte baptism as a way of associating themselves with the Jewish faith. For a further discussion of each use of Jewish ritual washing, see Martin, *Exploring Bible Times*, 86–90.

7. Mishnah, *Aboth* 5:21.

8. Of the 165 uses of the term "Jordan River" in the Old Testament, 117 deal with the notion of crossing a boundary. Henry O. Thompson, "Jordan River," *Anchor Bible Dictionary*, ed. D. N. Freedman (New York: Anchor, 1992), 3:954.

9. This summary is based on Jeremias, *Jerusalem in the Time of Jesus*, 235–36.

10. No principle was more firmly established than that authoritative teaching required the endorsement of one already in authority. Edersheim, *Life and Times of Jesus the Messiah*, 2:381–82.

11. The hometown of Mary, Martha, and Lazarus is also called Bethany, but that town was located near Jerusalem (John 11:1, 18). A different Bethany, Bethany of Perea, also existed. It was located on the other side of the Jordan River, about four and a half miles north of the Dead Sea. Finegan, *Archeology of the New Testament*, 13.

12. The proposed location of Jesus's stay in the Wilderness of Judea is northwest of Old Testament Jericho where Byzantine Christians built a church on a mountain called Jebel Quarantal (Mount of the Forty). McRay, *Archaeology and the New Testament*, 161–62.

13. Edersheim, *Life and Times of Jesus the Messiah*, 1:439. See also, for example, Matt. 5:1; 26:55; John 8:2.

14. Finegan, *Archeology of the New Testament*, 97. Jesus instructed his disciples to obey the teachings of Pharisees when they sat in the Seat of Moses (Matt. 23:1–3).

15. Josephus, *J. W.* 1.16.4.

16. For a further discussion of this foreign occupation, see Martin, *Exploring Bible Times*, 103–4.

17. Mendel Nun, *The Sea of Galilee and Its Fishermen in the New Testament* (Israel: Kibbutz Ein Gev, 1993), 28.

18. Mendel Nun, "Cast Your Nets upon the Waters: Fish and Fishermen in Jesus's Time," *Biblical Archaeology Review* 19 (November–December 1993): 53–55.

19. In addition, Hellenized Jews dominated the west and northeast of the Sea of Galilee. Martin, *Exploring Bible Times*, 99.

20. To learn more about the archaeology of the first-century synagogue at Capernaum, see McRay, *Archaeology and the New Testament*, 163–64.

21. Edersheim, *Life and Times of Jesus the Messiah*, 1:437.

22. Examples in rabbinic literature of rabbis doing miracles include Rabbi Honi HaMe'aggel (Talmud, *Taanit* 19a) and Rabbi HaNinah Ben Dosa (Talmud, *Berakhot* 34b).

23. "Son of Man" was a title for the Messiah (Dan. 7:13–14). Healing works were associated with the coming of the Messiah (Isa. 61:1–2; see also Luke 4:18–21).

24. This home was likely an *insula* home. Such homes were constructed of local basalt and built according to a common floor plan. A larger courtyard was surrounded by a set of smaller rooms, all with doorways that opened into this central courtyard. See McRay, *Archaeology and the New Testament*, 81.

25. The "house of Peter" lies just a few yards away from the synagogue in Capernaum. Finegan, *Archeology of the New Testament*, 107–10.

26. The region northwest of the Sea of Galilee was dominated by an observant Jewish presence. Martin, *Exploring Bible Times*, 99.

27. Graham Webster, *The Roman Imperial Army of the First and Second Centuries*, 3rd ed. (New York: Barnes & Noble, 1979), 12. Originally centurions commanded units of one hundred men, but after the Marian reforms (ca. 107 BC) most centurions controlled units of eighty men.

28. Witherington, *New Testament History*, 117.

29. Edersheim, *Life and Times of Jesus the Messiah*, 1:549–50.

30. Mishnah, *Sheqalim* 4:1, 3–4.

31. Josephus, *Antiquities* (hereafter *Ant.*) 14.7.2.

32. Most other English translations (i.e., NASB, NRSV, NKJV) state that Peter was to throw in a line with a "hook"—which may have been a grappling hook—and then look into the mouth of the first fish he caught.

33. These fish congregate near the shore in order to spawn. Once the eggs have been fertilized, they carry the eggs in their mouths for two to three weeks until they hatch. They are known to pick up items and carry them in their mouths just before spawning. For a further discussion, see Nun, *Sea of Galilee and Its Fishermen*, 6–7.

Part 3 Jesus's Parables and Teaching

1. The Hebrew name for the city is *Migdal Nuniya* (Babylonian Talmud, *Pesahim* 46a); Josephus calls it *Taricheae* (*J. W.* 2.21.3–4). The Hellenized Jews were those who adapted to Greek culture, and the fact that Magdala had both a synagogue and a hippodrome speaks to the Hellenized nature of the Jews living there. Josephus, *J. W.* 2.21.3–4.

2. Anson F. Rainey and R. Steven Notley, *The Sacred Bridge: Carta's Atlas of the Biblical World* (Jerusalem: Carta, 2006), 355.

3. The practice is still used today in certain villages in the Holy Land.

4. Murphy-O'Connor, *The Holy Land*, 429.

5. For a discussion of roadways and transportation, see John A. Beck, "Travel and Transportation," in *The Land of Milk and Honey: An Introduction to the Geography of Israel* (St. Louis: Concordia, 2006), 171–80.

6. Josephus, *Life* 2:10.

7. The school of Shammai considered it important to follow the *letter of the law* while those of Hillel generally held to the *spirit of the law*. For example, "The School of Shammai say: . . . Nets may not be set out for wild animals [on a Friday] . . . unless there is time for them to be caught the same day [prior to the coming of Sabbath]. And the School of Hillel permit it." *Shabbat* 1:6b.

8. They criticized Jesus for eating with tax collectors and sinners (Matt. 9:11), and they said he was driving out demons with the help of the prince of demons (Matt. 9:34).

9. Edersheim, *Life and Times of Jesus the Messiah*, 2:52.

10. The discussion of what constituted work was represented in the Mishnah. The debated activities include: the extinguishing of a lamp (*Shabbat* 2:5), the amount of wood one could gather (*Shabbat* 12:2), the number of letters that could be written (*Shabbat* 12:3), and the type of knot one could tie (*Shabbat* 15:1).

11. *Shabbat* 7:2.

12. "A great general rule have they laid down concerning the Sabbath: . . . If he knew that it was Sabbath . . . If he committed many acts of work of one main class, he is liable only to one Sin-offering." *Shabbat* 7:1. "R. Akiba said: I asked R. Eliezer, If a man did many acts of work . . . on many Sabbaths . . . what happens?—is he liable to one [Sin-offering] for all of them?" *Kerithoth* 3:10.

13. "These are they that are to be stoned. . . . he that profanes the Sabbath." Mishnah, *Sanhedrin* 7:4.

14. Josephus pictured every patch of land in the Galilee as cultivated land. *J. W.* 3.3.2.

15. K. C. Hanson and Douglas E. Oakman, *Palestine in the Time of Jesus* (Minneapolis: Fortress Press, 1998), 104.

16. Making use of fertilizer and mechanized planting, plowing, and harvesting, farmers in Israel today can produce a yield forty times what was sown. Ibid., 105.

17. Martin, *Exploring Bible Times*, 99.

18. Nun, *Sea of Galilee and Its Fishermen*, 28–34.

19. Ibid., 16.

20. This description of the seine net (dragnet) and manner of fishing with that kind of net is derived from Nun, "Cast Your Net upon the Waters," 51–52.

21. These men would go so far as to rebuke those who brought their children to Jesus so he could lay his hands on them (Matt. 19:13). The increase of a person's value with age is implied in Mishnah, *Abot* 5:21.

22. In this instance, a child remains the focus of the parable because the lost sheep is equated with a child. Jesus uses the same parable in a different setting to affirm the value of tax collectors and sinners when he is criticized for spending time with them (Luke 15:1–7). In both cases, the parable affirms the value of all people no matter how they are valued by society.

23. They were raised for their food value, for their wool, and for sacrifices to the Lord. For a further discussion, see George Cansdale, *All the Animals of the Bible Lands* (Grand Rapids: Zondervan, 1970), 48–56.

24. McRay, *Archaeology and the New Testament*, 77–78, 80–82.

25. Josephus, *Ant.* 16:3.

26. "If a man said, 'I will sin and repent, and sin again and repent', he will be given no chance to repent. [If he said] 'I will sin and the Day of Atonement will effect atonement', then the Day of Atonement effects no atonement. For transgressions that are between man and God the Day of Atonement effects atonement, but for transgressions that are between a man and his fellow the Day of Atonement effects only if he has appeased his fellow." Mishnah, *Yoma* 8:9.

27. Significant tensions and even hostility existed between Jews and Samaritans in the first century (John 4:9). Josephus speaks of incidents in which the Samaritans attacked and injured Jews who were passing through Samaria on their way to the festivals in Jerusalem. *J. W.* 2.12.3; *Ant.* 20.6.1.

28. In the Old Testament this road is called the Arabah Road (2 Kings 25:4; Jer. 39:4; 52:7). It appears that the later Roman road follows the same route that had been in use for centuries. David A. Dorsey, *The Roads and Highways of Ancient Israel*, ASOR Library of Biblical and Near Eastern Archaeology (Baltimore: Johns Hopkins University Press, 1991), 204–6.

29. The region generally receives less than eight inches of annual precipitation. What rain does fall quickly runs off the marl-coated slopes cascading toward the Dead Sea.

30. Edersheim, *Life and Times of Jesus the Messiah*, 2:183–84.

31. See David's experience with predators related in 1 Sam. 17:34–37.

32. One of the most stinging criticisms God leveled at the corrupt religious leaders of the Old Testament was when he called them abusive shepherds (Ezekiel 34).

33. Edersheim, *Life and Times of Jesus the Messiah*, 2:466.

34. Josephus, *J. W.* 1.14.4; *Ant.* 14.14.4. Witherington, *New Testament History*, 54–55.

35. Jesus was at the home of Zacchaeus in Jericho when he told this parable (see Luke 19).

36. McRay, *Archaeology and the New Testament*, 133–36.

37. See Mark 7:24; Luke 10:5; 19:5; John 12:1.

38. Philip J. King and Lawrence E. Stager, *Life in Biblical Israel*, Library of Ancient Israel (Louisville: Westminster John Knox, 2001), 39.

39. Mishnah, *Baba Bathra* 6:4.

40. Thus great risk attended a household that was divided (Matt. 12:25), explaining the great burden the disciples of Jesus took on by leaving a household for the sake of following him (Matt. 19:29).

41. King and Stager, *Life in Biblical Israel*, 39–40.

42. Athalya Brenner and Jan Willem van Henten, eds., *Food and Drink in the Biblical Worlds*, Semeia (Society of Biblical Literature) 86 (1999): 22.

43. Matthews and Benjamin, *Social World of Ancient Israel*, 47.

44. Brenner and van Henten, eds., *Food and Drink in the Biblical Worlds*, 26.

Part 4 Jesus in the World of the Gentiles

1. The Greek word *sēmeion* is repeatedly used by the Septuagint translators in reference to the initial signs Moses used before the elders of Israel and the Egyptian pharaoh (Exod. 4:8–9, 17, 28, 30) as well as when speaking about the plagues God leveled against Egypt when they refused to release the Israelites (Exod. 10:1–2; 11:9–10; Deut. 4:34; 7:19; 26:8; 29:3; 34:11).

2. Gath Hepher was on the northern side of this ridge, while Nazareth was located three miles away on the south side. Martin, *Exploring Bible Times*, 95.

3. Jonah served as a prophet during the days of Jeroboam II (see 2 Kings 14:25–29).

4. John uses the Greek word *dei* to express the necessity of this particular move.

5. The social tension between those who were pure blood descendants of Abraham and those of mixed descent rose and fell during the biblical period. Jeremias, *Jerusalem in the Time of Jesus*, 354. The fact that in spite of the ethnic tension the Jews still traveled on the road through Samaria is supported by the Gospel accounts (Luke 9:52–53) and reports from Josephus, *J. W.* 2.12.3; *Ant.* 20.6.1.

6. For a further discussion of the demographics around the Sea of Galilee, see Martin, *Exploring Bible Times*, 99.

7. James Martin, "Crossing Enemy Lines," *TableTalk* (Ligonier Ministries), May 1990, 34–35.

8. Nun, *Sea of Galilee and Its Fishermen*, 54.

9. E.g., Matt. 4:15; 10:5, 18; 20:19, 25.

10. The large crowd that had gathered to hear Jesus speak may well have done so after hearing the witness of the formerly demon-possessed man he had healed. That man had asked to accompany Jesus but was told instead to remain and tell others about his experience (Mark 5:18–20).

11. Leland Ryken, James C. Wilhoit, and Tremper Longman III, eds., "Seven," in *Dictionary of Biblical Imagery* (Downers Grove, IL: InterVarsity Press, 1998), 774–75.

12. Edersheim, *Life and Times of Jesus the Messiah*, 1:679–80.

13. For further discussion, see David G. Hansen, *In Their Sandals: How His Followers Saw Jesus* (Longwood, FL: Xulon Press, 2007), 33–40.

14. Martin, *Exploring Bible Times*, 122.

15. Caesarea Philippi is different from Caesarea Maritima, the port city on the Mediterranean Sea that was built by Herod the Great.

16. For more on Bashan, see Carl G. Rasmussen, *NIV Atlas of the Bible* (Grand Rapids: Zondervan, 1989), 29–30.

17. McRay, *Archaeology and the New Testament*, 173.

18. LaMoine F. DeVries, "Caesarea Philippi," in *Cities of the Biblical World* (Peabody, MA: Hendrickson, 1997), 266.

19. Eusebius, *History*, 7.17.301.

20. James and John had just been with Jesus during his transfiguration. During that experience, they had seen Elijah (Luke 9:28–36).

21. Since Ahaziah clearly expected them to return from Ekron with an answer, his surprise must relate to the fact that they had returned so quickly (2 Kings 1:1–5).

22. The Samaritans were people of mixed Gentile and Jewish bloodlines whose theology was similar but not identical to the theology of the Jews. The first century was a time of embittered relationships between these two ethnic groups. See Jeremias, *Jerusalem in the Time of Jesus*, 352–58.

23. In addition to the illustration that follows, Jesus tells a story about a Samaritan who befriends an injured Jew on the road to Jericho (Luke 10:25–37). He also rebuked James and John when they wished to call down fire on a Samaritan village (Luke 9:51–56).

24. The road to Dothan formed part of the border between Samaria and Galilee.

25. Medieval reports place this miracle at Ginae (modern-day Jenin). George Turner, *Historical Geography of the Holy Land* (Grand Rapids: Baker, 1973), 121. This may in part be associated with the observation that Ginae is located on the border between Samaria and Galilee. See Josephus, *Ant.* 20.6.1. Ginae is just a short distance from Dothan, a location associated with Elisha (2 Kings 6:13). See Hansen, *In Their Sandals*, 55–59.

26. Murphy-O'Connor, *The Holy Land*, 412.

27. Josephus, *Ant.* 18.2.1; *J. W.* 2.18.11; 3.2.4.

28. See Josephus, *Life* 12; *J. W.* 2.21.6.

Part 5 Jesus in and around Jerusalem

1. Jeremias, *Jerusalem in the Time of Jesus*, 198.

2. Edersheim, *Life and Times of Jesus the Messiah*, 1:370–71.

3. Josephus, *J. W.* 5.5.2.

4. Josephus, *Ant.* 15.11.4–5.

5. Eilat Mazar, *The Complete Guide to the Temple Mount Excavations* (Jerusalem: Shoham Academic Research and Publication, 2002), 33–34.

6. There are some exceptions where we find "the Jews" used in a generic sense. For example, Jesus speaks to the woman in John 4:22 and announces, "Salvation is from the Jews."

7. There is some uncertainty about the name of the pools due to the variety of names offered in the Greek manuscripts of John. Yet the best support is for the

name Bethesda. For a discussion of the evidence, see Finegan, *Archeology of the New Testament*, 228–29.

8. The northern of the two pools may be the same as the Upper Pool (2 Kings 18:17; Isa. 7:3) in existence during the days of the Divided Kingdom. The southern pool may have been added by the high priest Simon in about 200 BC (*Sirach* 50:3). Murphy-O'Connor, *The Holy Land*, 28–29.

9. Edersheim, *The Temple*, 275.

10. Mishnah, *Sukkah* 4:9.

11. Mishnah, *Sukkah* 3:9.

12. Prophets such as Isaiah and Micah prophesied of Jesus being the Messiah (see Isa. 9:1–7; Mic. 5:2).

13. Edersheim, *Life and Times of Jesus the Messiah*, 1:225.

14. Ibid.

15. Jeremias, *Jerusalem in the Time of Jesus*, 72, 267.

16. For an analysis of this event, see Hansen, *In Their Sandals*, 67–73.

17. For an overview of the traditional Jewish perspective, see Edersheim, *Life and Times of Jesus the Messiah*, 2:178–79.

18. Josephus, *J. W.* 5.5.1.

19. Ibid., 5.5.2.

20. This festival is also called the Feast of Lights or Hanukkah.

21. For the Messiah's role in restoration of worship, see Martin, *Exploring Bible Times*, 42–43.

22. This route was already in use during Old Testament times and had been improved as part of the Roman road system during the first century. See Dorsey, *Roads and Highways of Ancient Israel*, 204–6.

23. On the palatial structures in New Testament Jericho, see McRay, *Archaeology and the New Testament*, 133–36.

24. Jews were required to pay a land tax, import and export taxes, and a personal head tax. Witherington, *New Testament History*, 86–87.

25. Jeremias, *Jerusalem in the Time of Jesus*, 310.

26. The oasis of Jericho nurtured a variety of income-producing trees like the balsam, sycamore, and palm. Edersheim, *Life and Times of Jesus the Messiah*, 2:350.

27. For an overview of the despised trades, see Jeremias, *Jerusalem in the Time of Jesus*, 303–12.

28. The prophet Amos emphasized his lowly origins in terms of his work as a shepherd and as a day laborer in the sycamore-fig plantations (Amos 7:14–15). Nogah Hareuveni, *Tree and Shrub in Our Biblical Heritage* (Kiryat Ono, Israel: Neot Kedumim, 1984), 91.

Part 6 Jesus Faces the Cross

1. Josephus, *J. W.* 2:411. "Men of power" were rich land owners.

2. Mishnah, *Yebamoth* 16:3. "Evidence [of the identity of a corpse] may be given only during the first three days [after death]; but R. Judah b. Baba says: [Decay in corpses is] not alike in all men, in all places, and at all times." Edersheim, *Life and Times of Jesus the Messiah*, 2:324–25.

3. For a discussion, see Martin, *Exploring Bible Times*, 161.

4. For a review of the location of Bethpage and the churches that have occupied this site, see Finegan, *Archeology of the New Testament*, 162–64.

5. Babylonian Talmud, *Menahot* 78b; Mishnah, *Menahot* 11:2.

6. Josephus, *Ant.* 18.2.2; Talmud, *Pesahim* 57a.

7. Many living in the first century believed that the faithful priest mentioned in 1 Sam. 2:35 was Zadok, a priest living at the time of David and Solomon (2 Sam. 8:17; 15:24; 1 Kings 1:8; 2:35). See Jeremias, *Jerusalem in the Time of Jesus*, 181–82.

8. Josephus, *Ant.* 18.4.3.

9. For a discussion of the preseason fig, see Michael Zohary, *Plants of the Bible* (Cambridge: Cambridge University Press, 1982), 58–59.

10. See part 5, note 24.

11. Josephus, *Ant.* 18.1.1.

12. For a description of the building, see Josephus, *J. W.* 5.5.8.

13. Josephus states that, following the practice of earlier Roman governors, Cumanus, a later Roman governor, ordered this very deployment. Josephus, *Ant.* 20.5.3.

14. The Temple proper was surrounded by a number of courts that increasingly limited access to segments of society the closer one got to it. Jewish men and women were allowed in this court, but not Gentiles (such as the Roman soldiers). The Court of Women functioned as the Temple treasury. For a discussion, see Finegan, *Archeology of the New Testament*, 194–96.

15. Edersheim, *Life and Times of Jesus the Messiah*, 2:387.

16. Even the rabbis taught that giving was from the heart. "It is said . . . to teach that it is all one whether a man offers much or little, if only he directs his mind towards heaven." Mishnah, *Menahoth* 13:11.

17. See 1 Kings 15:13; 2 Kings 23:4, 6, 12; 2 Chron. 15:16; 29:16; 30:14.

18. See 2 Chron. 22:10–23:15; *Ant.* 9.7.3.

19. This prophecy included a warning fulfilled with the pouring out of the Holy Spirit (Joel 2:28–32; Matt. 24:29; Acts 2:17–21) and the destruction of the Temple in AD 70 (Dan. 9:27; 11:31; 12:11; Matt. 24:15–21).

Part 7 The Arrest and Trials of Jesus

1. This reconstruction of the Passover (Last Supper of Jesus) is taken from Edersheim, *Life and Times of Jesus the Messiah*, 2:492–95. For further information on the reconstruction of the Passover, see www.biblicalresources.net.

2. John is not directly identified as the one reclining on Jesus's chest. The Greek, NASB, NIV, King James, ASV, and other translations state that the disciple whom Jesus loved was reclining on his chest. Many maintain that disciple is John (see John 19:26; 20:2; 21:7, 20).

3. Edersheim, *Life and Times of Jesus the Messiah*, 2:494–95.

4. Concerning the authority of rabbis: "Rabbi, tell us the two or three things which you stated [formerly] on your father's authority." Babylonian Talmud, *Shabbat* 15a. "He shall loosen all the fetters which bind them that is in his Congregation." *The Damascus Rule* xiii.10. G. Vermes, *The Dead Sea Scrolls in English*, 3rd ed. (New York: Penguin Books, 1987), 97.

5. For a discussion of the rare phenomenon of hemohidrosis, see William D. Edwards, Wesley J. Gabel, and Floyd E. Hosmer, "On the Physical Death of Jesus," *Journal of the American Medical Association* 255, no. 11 (March 21, 1986): 1456.

6. John gives us this man's name: Malchus. The Hebrew equivalent may be "counselor." See Edersheim, *Life and Times of Jesus the Messiah*, 2:544.

7. Josephus, *Ant.* 20.8.8.

8. Josephus, *J. W.* 1.13.9.

9. Martin, *Exploring Bible Times*, 176.

10. For a thorough treatment of the attempt, see Finegan, *Archeology of the New Testament*, 242–45.

11. Josephus locates the house of Ananias (i.e., Annas) the high priest in this part of Jerusalem. *J. W.* 2.17.6. But the context of the event may place the "courtyard" within the Temple complex.

12. McRay, *Archaeology and the New Testament*, 78.

13. Mishnah, *Sukkah* 5:4; *Tamid* 1:2; *Yomah* 1:8. A stone that had tumbled from the southwestern corner of the Temple complex bears the paraphrased inscription, "To the place of trumpeting." In its original location, high above the central valley, it marked the spot where the priest sounded the trumpet. Mazar, *Guide to the Temple Mount Excavations*, 42–45.

14. Mishnah, *Arakhin* 9:3.

15. Mishnah, *Arakhin* 9:4.

16. This chapter follows the position of Jeremias, *Jerusalem in the Time of Jesus*, 139–40.

17. Acts 1:18 says that Judas bought the field. The chief priests regarded this money as continuing to belong to Judas. From the perspective of Acts, the chief priests purchased the land, but they did so with Judas's money.

18. Those bringing coins to the Temple as an offering placed them in one of thirteen trumpet-shaped boxes, each of which was designated for a specific cause. Edersheim, *Life and Times of Jesus the Messiah*, 2:387.

19. Jeremias, *Jerusalem in the Time of Jesus*, 140.

20. With some exceptions, cemeteries were located outside the city walls.

21. For a further discussion, see Finegan, *Archeology of the New Testament*, 245–46.

22. This palace was much more luxurious than the Antonia Fortress. Josephus was overwhelmed by the beautiful groves, gardens, canals, art, and architecture. Josephus, *J. W.* 5.4.4. Philo notes that this was Pilate's residence of choice while in Jerusalem. Philo, *The Embassy of Gaius*, par. 38.

23. Edersheim, *The Temple*, 89.

24. Priests who had been defiled could not offer sacrifices. "They [the priests] were like them that have a blemish: they may share and they may eat [of the holy things] but they may not offer sacrifices." Mishnah, *Menahoth* 13:12.

25. For further information on Jewish law concerning uncleanness of Gentile homes and how entering a Gentile home made a Jew unclean, see: Mishnah, *Ohalot* 18:7, 10; Mishnah, *Kelim* 1:4; Josephus, *Ant.* 18.4.3.

26. Josephus, *J. W.* 1.6.1; 1.7.2.

27. Philo, *Embassy of Gaius*, 299–300, 305.

28. Josephus, *Ant.* 18:55.

29. The judge's seat was most likely set up in front of Herod's palace, which was the palace that served as the residence for Pilate while he was in Jerusalem. In a later instance we see Florus living in the same residence and setting up his judge's seat in the same location. Josephus, *J. W.* 2.14.8.

30. For a further discussion of a Roman trial, see Witherington, *New Testament History*, 152.

31. Mishnah, *Sotah* 9:6.

32. Martin, *Exploring Bible Times*, 186–87.

33. Pilate had murdered Galileans while they were making sacrifices at the altar in the Temple (Luke 13:1–2). He also sought to abolish Jewish laws and brought offensive images into Jerusalem. And after taking money from the Temple treasury for a public works project, he violently quelled the ensuing uprising. Josephus, *Ant.* 18.3.1–2.

34. Philo, *Embassy of Gaius*, par. 38.

35. Josephus, *Ant.* 18.4.2.

36. Martin, *Exploring Bible Times*, 187.

Part 8 The Crucifixion, Resurrection, and Ascension of Jesus

1. Murphy-O'Connor, *The Holy Land*, 45–48. Based on Matt. 27:33 and presuming that Calvary was a hill that resembled a skull, Gordon popularized a location now known as Gordon's Calvary. McRay, *Archaeology and the New Testament*, 206–16.

2. The exception was the tombs of the Davidic dynasty, which were allowed within the city walls of Jerusalem.

3. Today the Church of the Holy Sepulcher is located within the Old City walls of Jerusalem. But prior to AD 41, this location was outside the city walls beyond the Gennath Gate. Josephus, *J. W.* 5.4.2.

4. Seneca, *De Ira III*, 19.2–20.1.

5. For another discussion of the two criminals with Jesus, see Hansen, *In Their Sandals*, 449–59.

6. Martin, *Exploring Bible Times*, 196.

7. Josephus, *Ant.* 13.14.2.

8. For a survey of those references, see Martin, *Exploring Bible Times*, 191–92.

9. Crucifixions are known that used a "T," an "X," or a "✝" shaped cross. Ibid., 192–94. And we know that Jesus was attached to the wood using nails because Thomas mentions the marks they left in his hands (John 20:25).

10. For a further discussion of the archaeological evidence and the various views on how the hands and feet were attached to the cross, see McRay, *Archaeology and the New Testament*, 204–6. The actual cause of death was hypovolemic shock or exhaustion asphyxia. Edwards, Gabel, and Hosmer, "On the Physical Death of Jesus Christ," 1461.

11. Mishnah, *Yoma* 5:1.

12. Edersheim, *Life and Times of Jesus the Messiah*, 2:611.

13. This is exactly what Jacob did when he received evidence (fraudulent as it was) that his son Joseph had been killed (Gen. 37:34).

14. Martin, *Exploring Bible Times*, 201.

15. Two locations that commemorate the site of Jesus's burial are the Garden Tomb (associated with Gordon's Calvary) and the Church of the Holy Sepulcher. See McRay, *Archaeology and the New Testament*, 206–17.

16. Mishnah, *Sanhedrin* 6:6.

17. The spices were not designed to embalm the body but to prevent toxic gases from forming in the sealed tomb. Martin, *Exploring Bible Times*, 204.

18. For an example of a square stone, see Martin, *Exploring Bible Times*, 202. For a round stone, see the discussion of the tomb of the Queen of Adiabene in Finegan, *Archeology of the New Testament*, 318.

19. The matter of reporting to the governor mentioned in Matthew 28:14 may have in view the general Roman protection offered to tombs as noted in the Nazareth Inscription.

20. Clyde E. Billington, "The Nazareth Inscription: Proof of the Resurrection of Christ" in *Artifacts* (Spring 2005): 17–21.

21. Quoted in Maier, *In the Fullness of Time*, 202.

22. According to the Mishnah, some families of priestly lineage came from Emmaus. "[They that played the instruments of music] were the slaves of the priests. . . . They were from the families of Beth ha-Pegarim and Beth Zipporya and from Emmaus, and they were eligible to give [their daughters] in marriage to priestly stock." *Kiddushin* 4:1. R. Hanina b. Anitgonus says they were Levites. Mishnah, *Arakhin* 2:4.

The site of ancient Emmaus has not been identified with certainty, and more than nine locations have been suggested. Hershel Shanks, "Emmaus Where Christ Appeared," *Biblical Archaeology Review* 34 (March/April 2008): 40–51. Also see, McRay, *Archaeology and the New Testament*, 221–22. Moreover, the Bible reports that Emmaus was "about seven miles from Jerusalem" (Luke 24:13)—close enough to walk there and return on the same day—which makes the claim that *Amwas* (Nicopolis) was twenty miles west of Jerusalem very problematic.

23. Since the fourth century, Christians have commemorated this event at churches erected on the northwest shore of the Sea of Galilee at Heptapegon (Seven Springs). Today the Chapel of the Primacy of St. Peter marks the spot. Finegan, *Archeology of the New Testament*, 92–94.

24. For a further discussion, see Martin, *Exploring Bible Times*, 103–4.

25. Murphy-O'Connor, *The Holy Land*, 124; Finegan, *Archeology of the New Testament*, 167–70.

SCRIPTURE INDEX

Dr. James C. Martin has an MDiv and a DMin in biblical studies. In 1980 and 1982–83 he worked on postgraduate studies in Jerusalem with Israeli scholars, focusing on the historical, cultural, and geographical context of the Bible, including archaeology and rabbinic studies. From 1983–89 he was program director and instructor at the Jerusalem Center for Biblical Studies, where he taught biblical studies on location throughout Israel. In 1989, Dr. Martin founded Bible World Seminars. Over the past twenty-five years he has had the opportunity to teach approximately 250 biblical overseas study programs throughout Israel, Egypt, Jordan, Turkey, and Greece to participants from numerous Christian colleges, seminaries, churches, and Christian organizations. He also offers seminars in the United States on the world of the Bible.

Dr. Martin and his wife, Stacey, are involved in aerial, land, museum, and nature photography and video filming throughout the Middle East and Europe, concentrating on the historical, geographical, cultural, and archaeological aspects of the Bible. Their photos appear in works such as the *Tyndale Illumina Bible*, the NIV *Archaeological Study Bible*, *The Zondervan Encyclopedia of the Bible*, *The Zondervan Dictionary of the Bible*, *Halley's Bible Handbook*, *The Bible in Ninety Days*, *A Visual Guide to Bible Events*, and numerous magazines and educational resources related to the world of the Bible. For more information, contact Dr. Martin at bibleworldseminars@gmail.com.

Dr. John Beck earned his PhD in theology (Hebrew and Old Testament) from Trinity International University in 1997. For sixteen years, he taught courses in Hebrew and Old Testament at various colleges and universities. During the last ten years, he has worked closely with Dr. James Martin both as a teacher in Israel and as a consultant for various publications.

Dr. Beck has studied the role of geography in biblical communication and has published articles in *JETS*, *SJOT*, *WTJ*, and *BibSac*. He also authored the article on geography for Baker's *Dictionary for Theological Interpretation of the Bible*. He recently published *The Land of Milk and Honey: An Introduction to the Geography of Israel* and *God as Storyteller: Seeking Meaning in Biblical Narrative*.

Colonel David G. Hansen, PhD, served in the US Army for thirty-five years. He taught at the US Army War College for nine years as chairman of the Department of National Security and Strategy and as a tenured professor who held the General Maxwell D. Taylor chair. He left active military service with academic degrees in geography (BA, University of Nebraska at Omaha) and international relations (MA, University of Texas). He then taught regional geography at Penn State for eight years while finishing his doctoral studies at Trinity Theological Seminary.

Hansen's on-site research in the Middle East includes extensive travel and participation in archaeological excavations. At the request of both the Israel Defense Forces and the Royal Jordanian Army, he was an academic consultant for the higher education of their professional military officers. He has published articles in several journals about the impact of geography on military affairs and the Bible, and has authored one book (*In Their Sandals: How His Followers Saw Jesus*) and contributed chapters to other books.

Hansen currently travels, writes, and teaches with Bible World Seminars and Youth With A Mission.